Strategic Psychotherapy

STRATEGIC PSYCHOTHERAPY

Brief and Symptomatic Treatment

RICHARD RABKIN

BASIC BOOKS, INC., PUBLISHERS

NEW YORK

79705

Library of Congress Cataloging in Publication Data

Rabkin, Richard, 1932–
  Strategic psychotherapy.

  Bibliographical References: p. 237
  Includes index.
  1. Psychotherapy. I. Title.
RC480.R32   616.8′914   76–43472
ISBN: 0–465–08217–3

TO

Miriam

David

AND

Jeffrey

CONTENTS

Epilogue
THE ENDGAME

APPENDIXES

ACKNOWLEDGMENTS

I AM TOLD that this book is likely to stir up controversy. In general, I think such controversy can have a beneficial effect if it is about the place of strategic psychotherapy within psychiatry, psychology, and psychotherapy. However, one type of controversy that I would like to minimize has to do with the origin of the ideas that I have attempted to integrate in this book. These ideas, like bubbles appearing on the surface of water heating over a fire, are appearing faster and faster and in many places at once. While brief, symptomatic treatment seems to be becoming a dominant movement and a force to be reckoned with (just as, in my analogy, one would soon expect the water to boil) there are bound to be concerns about priorities and the origin of ideas. Any strategic therapist worth his salt is sensitive to the beneficial political consequences of priority when a significant movement develops. Therefore, rather than precipitate or get caught in internecine battles, I would like to make clear both the history of the movement as I know it and my indebtedness to those from whom I learned.

My training began at the William Alanson White Institute when Clara Thompson was the director; I remained there for the short period when Meyer Maskin, my analyst, replaced her. At the time, it was a place at which one could become acquainted with social psychology and American pragmatism. I was particularly influenced by the philosopher Justus Buchler who presented Pierce, Dewey, Mead, and to some extent British

linguistic philosophy. These philosophical positions are ultimately behaviorist in orientation, and Maskin presented them in
relation to Harry Stack Sullivan's work in a transactional and
behavioral framework that foreshadowed much current thinking.
For me this was and is my theoretical base.

Upon my return from the Air Force, the White Institute had
changed to a more mentalistic, psychoanalytic orientation, and
the ideas I had learned there were now heretical. Although
branded as a heretic, I was graciously directed by the White
Institute to the group formed at Wiltwyck School for Boys,
which included Edgar H. Auerswald and Salvador Minuchin. It
was from them that I learned of family therapy, ecology, and
systems theory. At the time, the other axis of family therapy was
in Palo Alto where Bateson, Jackson, Haley, Weakland, and
others worked. Although the double bind theory dealt with philosophy and communication and therefore seemed germane, it
was the work of Jay Haley exposing power and influence as an
issue, and his candid discussions of manipulating patients with or
without double binds that was probably the most significant for
me at the time. Haley's influence has been truly seminal, and
this book owes much to his pathbreaking efforts. For me, it
broke out of the "explaining" set that we had developed (we
explained things with systems theory) and moved in the direction of strategic action. Gillis' work on "social influence therapy" seems a logical extension of Haley.

The practical question for followers of Haley is, if the patient
is to be openly influenced, in what way should a therapist proceed? Jerome Frank's work introduced me to the problem of
demoralization and control of the patient's expectations, issues I
deal with in the opening sections of this book.

The next significant step for me was the Palo Alto clinicians'
work (Watzlawick, Fisch, Weakland, Bodin, etc.) at the Brief
Therapy Center. They clearly emphasized that it is the patient's
own strategy that must be modified, not his symptoms, and this

pathbreaking work held for me the same excitement that Haley's earlier work did. This book could not have been written without their contributions.

Hypnosis interpreted as an influencing ceremony has always been a prominent feature of the work in the area I describe. For example, Haley introduced Milton Erickson's work to a wide audience. I have always considered Erickson's hypnotic treatments as models to study and attempt to understand. In addition, I have had the good fortune to take Herbert Spiegel's courses on his hypnotic method. I believe that he is the originator of the concentration model of hypnosis, which is becoming more and more popular as his work becomes better known. It is replacing the sleep model, as the sleep model replaced the attack model. Several of the clinical examples which I cite in the text were first encountered in his course. Spiegel also stresses the concept of ceremonial healing which seems to have had its origin in anthropology with Levi-Strauss' comparison of witch-doctors to psychoanalysts, a theme that is further developed by E. Fuller Torrey.

The work of Hansell on crisis intervention, Coyne on depression, and Lemert on paranoia have also been important influences on me.

Of course, there are many others mentioned in the text who have made important contributions. The selection of material, critical remarks, and a few additions of my own, are, however, my sole responsibility.

As a social psychiatrist, I believe that knowledge is infectious, and it is difficult to know where one has caught it, whether it will have a permanent effect, or whether one can grow out of it to believe an alternative theory, even while those *you* have infected remain under the influence. Acknowledging the source of one's own infection is easy, but writing history is difficult. We are all carriers; no one is the beginning. Knowledge is the product of qualities inherent in the system. It is only the ignorant

man, misled by personal egotism, who says, "I am the source."
As G. H. Mead expressed it, history is only the propaganda of
the present, written to substantiate a particular political view.

My beliefs, then, make me acutely aware of my indebtedness
and, at the same time, move me to encourage the reader to be
cautious and critical.

New York City, 1976

Strategic Psychotherapy

INTRODUCTION

Standing on One Leg

Wisdom is knowing others;
Enlightenment is knowing the self;
Mastering others requires force;
Mastering the self requires strength.

Lao Tsu

THIS BOOK is a guide for the psychotherapist, beginning or advanced, who seeks an integrated discussion of brief, symptomatic psychotherapy which is not merely an abbreviated form of the psychodynamic therapy which he already knows. It is not a manual in the sense of being a little book one can slip into one's hip pocket in order to follow distinct protocols—although in several Appendixes I have included verbatim illustrations of certain techniques to be sure the reader has understood what is being presented in the text. I hope that after finishing this book the reader will be equipped to develop a personal method of his own and to know in what further directions he would choose to travel. Above all, I hope there will be no mysteries. Too often in the past, brief, symptomatic treatment has been illustrated by the work of intuitive, talented, but inimitable therapists whose own impressive cases sound like plots from the television series *Mission Impossible*. Take as an example the incident in which Milton Erickson (1964a) was flown to South America to demonstrate and lecture on hypnosis before a distinguished audience. As he was lecturing he was introduced to a volunteer, a nurse, whom he was to hypnotize. The only problem was that she spoke no English and Erickson speaks no Spanish. Erickson's solution, using sign language, was ingenious, but it is not the sort that can be copied. Such illustrations, which have been unfortunately common in the area of symptomatic treatment, are impressive but not enlightening. Furthermore, the situations in which they are necessary are not likely to occur in one's practice. My intention here is to present every case illustration, every technique in such a manner that the reader can understand it and, if he were so tempted, employ it himself in the everyday course of his practice.

As a guide, this book attempts to place within a framework a great many practices and approaches, but there is no claim to comprehensive coverage. To accomplish this, given the proliferation of new techniques, a monthly newsletter would be required. Instead, I hope that the reader will explore in more detail those techniques which I mention briefly. In addition, when he comes across something new and not specifically discussed in the text (for example, nude group therapy in swimming pools), I hope he will not simply dismiss it as a typical example of West Coast lunacy and wild psychotherapy, but be able confidently to identify the variations on old themes that he has read about here.

I have tried not to imply that strategic psychotherapy is itself a modality, a specific technique. I believe the state of the art of psychotherapy is such that no one need, or for that matter should, practice one technique exclusively, whether it is hypnosis, family therapy, or psychodynamic psychotherapy. One ought to be able to use each of these as warranted by the occasion. I believe that those trained in a single modality, or trained to regard a single modality as superior to all others, will tend to fit the patient to the Procrustean bed, rather than attempt to determine what characteristics of the situation suggest what therapy. At the same time, certain generalizations can be made about strategic psychotherapy. In order to locate a great many techniques in a coherent framework it is necessary to view them from some terra firma.

THE FRAMEWORK OF STRATEGIC PSYCHOTHERAPY

It is said that two Talmud scholars were asked by a Russian general to identify the essence of the religion he found himself persecuting so zealously. The general was only mildly curious and demanded an answer that could be delivered "while standing on one leg," that is, in a sentence. The first scholar found the task too great for him. The second scholar, Hillel, answered, "Do not do unto others as you would not wish them to do unto you. All the rest is commentary."

Were I asked to explain strategic psychotherapy standing on one leg—which in some ways is the task of an introduction—I would answer, "Patients attempt to master their problems with a strategy which, because it is unsuccessful, the therapist changes. All the rest is commentary."

In this book, using Lao Tsu's terminology quoted earlier, the reader is presented with methods of influencing others and of teaching patients how to master themselves. Let us take cigarette smoking as an example. It is a known health hazard which many people find difficult to terminate. Between 1966 and 1970 an estimated 22 million American smokers made at least one serious but unsuccessful attempt to quit smoking. Although the government requires that cigarettes be clearly labeled a health hazard, more cigarettes are currently being sold in the United States than ever before. Were a patient in therapy to seek "wisdom" about cigarette smoking, he would discover why people, in general, smoke. If he sought "enlightenment," he would discover why he, in particular, smoked. Neither of these tasks is the goal of strategic therapy. On the other hand, if a public health official were seeking to prevent others from smoking—seeking force, in Lao Tsu's terms—or if he himself wished to stop smoking—seeking strength—then both of these latter tasks are within the scope of strategic therapy.

Strategies used by patients and therapists alike fall into two categories. First are those home remedies or commonsense solutions that have stood the test of time—spanking a child if he is bad, for example—which seem to work on most occasions. Second are those solutions that do not seem to make common sense, crazy ideas that "just might work"—instead of spanking a child one might encourage him to repeat what he has done. An example of this opens chapter 6 on reverse psychology. Here the problem is with a four-year-old boy who has daily temper tantrums. The commonsense solutions were tried and failed. The therapist suggested that the child continue to have temper tantrums, with the slight modification that they occur in a "tantrum place." This odd strategy succeeded quickly and efficiently in terminating the tantrums. This book is about the second category of strategies: uncommonsense.

In a manner of speaking, uncommonsense therapies (Haley 1973a) can be seen as including organic treatments like the major tranquilizers as well as psychoanalytically oriented therapies. The former concentrate on the brain while the latter focus on the mind. This book is about a third category of uncommonsense therapy which focuses on transactions between people. In a sense it is a behavioral approach. Behavioral approaches are divided into two schools which, for want of a better descriptive shorthand, can be referred to as the humorless school and the humorous school. There is something humorous about the strategy that the therapist took in the treatment of the four-year-old with temper tantrums. The classical (humorless) use of learning theory, which is more frequently seen as behavioral therapy or behavior modification, is referred to but not discussed in detail in this book. However, since transactions between people constitute behavior, both approaches are called behaviorist.

Much of the orientation of strategic psychotherapy came from the same matrix that spawned family therapy and crisis intervention, and for a while it was appropriate to use these terms for the same material. However, both family therapy and crisis intervention have "suffered" from becoming a successful part of psychodynamic psychiatry. That is, families and crisis situations are now seen from the same point of view as individual patients whose therapists are concentrating on offering them insights or interpretations. As these two disciplines became more "establishment," they lost their distinctive characteristics. In an effort to underscore the fact that there is a therapy that does not seek wisdom and enlightenment, I find that the term "strategic psychotherapy" seems best suited to remain a distinct entity. An alternative that I considered was "prescriptive psychotherapy" —since it is customary in this therapy to offer the patient a task to perform—but I have rejected this alternative predominantly because the term "strategic psychotherapy" is already in use thanks to the pioneering work of Jay Haley (1963). Strategic psychotherapy is usually brief compared with psychoanalysis, but "brief therapy" as a term is not specific enough.

In short, then, this book is about changing the approach that patients take toward their problems and symptoms. It is not about commonsense solutions, modifications of body chemistry, the unconscious or motivational determinants of behavior, or behavior modification.

Like a chess game, the book is divided into three phases: the opening, the midgame, and the endgame. As in chess, the opening is deemed the crucial part of therapy. Chapter 1 is about the characteristics of the patient, notably the fact that patients come to doctors and therapists when they are demoralized, not merely when they have problems. Chapter 2 concerns the importance of first getting patients to believe that they can achieve their goal, whatever it may be; chapter 3 is about compliance; and chapter 4 concerns hypnosis and imagery.

The chapters that comprise the section on the midgame

include discussions of relaxation, reverse psychology, symptom transfer, and working with more than one patient at a time (what used to be considered family therapy).

Exiting is discussed in the final chapter. There are several Appendixes detailing certain procedures (for example, hypnotic induction) which did not seem appropriate for expansion within the text.

Several factors influence the response of a psychotherapist to strategic treatment. Dr. Donald Light, Jr. (1975), a research sociologist and professor at Princeton, studied residents at the largest of Harvard's training facilities and found that they conformed to three basic types which he called therapeutic, managerial, and cognitive. Therapeutic residents "want very much to help their patients. Ideologically, they are open-minded and eclectic. They will employ whatever techniques promise results." Managerial residents "did not become nearly so emotional about their patients and from the start they preferred administrative techniques of therapy. On the hospital patients, they used restrictions, drugs, ECT, perhaps behavioral therapy, and they organized a therapeutic milieu for the patients with nurses and attendants. In short, they managed their patients." The third type, or cognitive resident, had usually gone to medical school in order to be a psychoanalyst, had not incorporated the medical model (i.e., strategic approaches), and did not expect to cure his patients. "Seemingly unaware of it, they talk about their patients as case studies in psychoanalytic theory and are very intellectual." Obviously, the cognitive type of resident will favor psychoanalytic treatment, the managerial type will be interested in strategies to the extent that prescription can be devised to deal with the "environment," and the therapeutic type presumably will be most receptive to my subsequent discussions.

With the success of prescriptive or strategic approaches there has been a tendency to mix prescriptive and interpretive techniques. The result has often been confusion. For example, in the area of sexual dysfunction a prescriptive approach has been pioneered by Masters and Johnson, and this has led to the widespread proliferation of sex clinics. Subsequently, clinicians have attempted to adapt the Masters and Johnson prescriptive approach to the framework of insight therapy. A director of a clinic for sexual dysfunctions has explained: "We teach patients sexual exercises [prescriptions] to remove the immediate anxieties and defenses that create and maintain their anti-erotic environment. We employ psychotherapy when deep anxieties or underlying pathologies impede our progress" (Kaplan 1974). I believe that this usage of psychological terms tends to blur the distinction between a prescriptive or strategic approach and an interpretive or psychodynamic one. Second, this statement suggests that one can fall back on psychodynamic psychotherapy when a strategic approach fails. I believe that this is misleading. At the very least, more precise criteria must be established to serve as a basis for the decision to use one technique or the other. Current practice is not to accept patients for psychodynamic psychotherapy *after* a strategic approach has failed. If anything, the situation is the reverse; after it can be shown that the patient understands the origins of his symptoms and they still persist, it is then assumed that they are residuals which can be treated with behavioral or strategic therapy. It certainly cannot be stated that psychoanalysis is a more powerful tool to be employed when there are difficulties with other approaches.

A study by Ursano and Dressler (1974) explored the rationale behind referring patients for brief therapy versus long-term therapy. Short-term therapy, lasting twelve sessions, was suggested in those cases in which the therapist felt that he understood the problem, and when the problem was focal in nature. If a problem could be dissected out, short-term therapy was the treatment of choice. Long-term therapy was suggested for problems which were confusing. The decision was not based on whether or not supportive or insight models were to be used. This is somewhat similar to the findings of Arnold Lazarus

(1971), who was surprised to discover that over twenty of his colleagues who consider themselves "behavior therapists" were undergoing psychoanalysis. These therapists were not suffering from focal problems. They felt that life held no meaning for them, or wished to be in better touch with their feelings.

I am of the opinion that if individual psychodynamic psychotherapy has taught us anything, it is how to interview patients at the outset of treatment. It has shown us that a patient's initial complaints may be misleading; that is, a nonsexual complaint (a woman who complains that she is obsessed with a man in her office) might hide a sexual dysfunction (lack of orgasms with her husband). For that matter, a man who consults a neurologist for headaches could have a sexual problem, and any patient might have a stake in sabotaging treatment, but such analyses constitute evaluation, not treatment.

While it is possible to use "dynamics" as a means of determining the point of entry for a strategy—in our examples, whether or not to attempt to prescribe for headache, obsession, or a sexual problem—frequently the word "dynamics" implies that the past is the critical factor to take into account. This has sent generations of psychiatrists scurrying back into the earliest years of a patient's life, usually following the formula that the more severe the problem, the earlier in the life of the patient one must investigate. However, what I have in mind when I say one should use dynamics at the outset to determine the point of entry is not adoption of a "strategy of reminiscence." I mean to suggest that knowledge of how people present their problems can help us determine whether to treat a patient for a headache (a pain syndrome) or for a sexual problem. What has come to be known as dynamics informs our history taking, not our therapy.

Finally, I would like to remind the reader that strategic psychotherapy is in its infancy. Compared with chess strategies, which have been recorded from the seventeenth century, our approaches should prompt considerable therapeutic humility. Although it is tempting to allow oneself to believe that there are powerful midgame strategies, and it is sometimes helpful to allow patients to do so, most of our therapeutic success can be attributed to the opening phases of psychotherapy. Therefore I caution the reader to study part 1 carefully before turning to the midgame. Successful therapy can occur from just utilizing the principles discussed in this section devoted to the opening. Like chess, the game is won or lost in the beginning.

Part One

THE OPENING

The beginning is halfway to the goal.
                              Oriental proverb

CHAPTER 1

Stone Soup:
The Patient's
Contribution to Therapy

BEFORE TURNING to a consideration of the goals and techniques of strategic psychotherapy, this chapter examines various characteristics of the patient—what he "brings" to therapy. The patient's attitudes and capacities, which he can contribute to the tasks of psychotherapy, are reminiscent of the guests' contributions to "stone soup" in the old Russian story. As the cook, the only ingredient you provide is a stone. To make this remarkably nutritious and filling food you boil the stone in a pot of water. Then you suggest to your guests that, although it would taste fine as it is, it would be even better if they happened to have an onion they could donate, as well as some parsley, tomatoes, meat, and so on. By the time you are done you can serve them, to their amazement and your credit, a remarkably good meal of stone soup.

In a recent case a depressed young woman came to see me and talked in the initial interview about her family and the difficulties she had had with them. As she left my office with her back turned to me, she mused that she was now going to look for a job suited to her interests and abilities. By so doing she was throwing the first ingredient into the pot. As McKinnon and Michels (1971) have pointed out, in emergency or crisis situations the patient will often fail to mention certain resources that he possesses or that are available. They believe that the patient does so because the need to appear helpless is unconsciously assumed to be the prerequisite to obtaining help. At such times the therapist must appear to be taking charge even if he has fewer resources at his command than does the patient. As in the recipe for stone soup, he must obtain the resources from the patient without appearing to do so. For example, a patient presents herself helplessly at an emergency room stating that her house has burned down. She must be helped to find a place to stay. The therapist states that he will help her, but does she just happen to have any ideas herself? She then tells him that she has a weekend house that is an hour's drive away. The therapist suggests that she go there for the time being; if she has any more difficulty, she is to call him.

The two examples just cited are rather simple and specific, but the process works on a more abstract level as well with "resources" such as hope. In order to understand the nature and origin of the ingredients of strategic psychotherapy, particularly those associated with the opening phase, it is necessary to clarify some of the more subtle and complex characteristics of the patient that can be useful or obstructive to the therapy.

CHARACTERISTICS OF THE PATIENT

HE IS WELL INFORMED

Years ago the disciplines of psychology and psychiatry encompassed a store of information which could only be obtained by personal consultation with a professional. Now, however, books on psychology and books offering advice for problems of a psychological nature are obtainable in supermarkets all over the United States. Colleges give courses in a wide range of problem-solving subjects from the now-traditional "Marriage and the Family" to modern courses on sex and drugs. In extension divisions there are many courses for nonmatriculated adults on subjects like marriage, being single, child rearing, self-discovery, and even preretirement planning.

The material presented in books and courses for the layman is often of good quality. A competent science writer who does research for a book or a college professor who has read extensively about one of these subjects can provide valid information to the public. Such a book or a course is not tailored to the particular problem of an individual patient, but most people probably can benefit from this inexpensive way of obtaining knowledge about whatever subject is a source of interest or difficulty to them.

Reading such a book or attending such a course is an extension of the commonsense approach of the average person when he has a problem: He gathers information about it. It was only an accident of the history of psychiatry that its context was unavailable to the average man in the street, and now for the most part this has been corrected. The patient now comes well informed. If he doesn't, there are numerous books or courses to which he can be referred, as well as some specialized group therapy techniques, such as awareness or assertiveness training, that are halfway between a course and a therapy experience. The fact that the patient is well informed or can be readily informed leads to a certain narrowing of the scope of psychotherapy.

A psychotherapist must have something more to offer than what commonsense information gathering can bring. This book is about uncommonsense psychiatry—those things at which common sense is not apt to arrive and which the patient probably cannot gather from a course or a book. Much that used to occupy a therapist's time (i.e., theoretical discussions) can now

be obtained "over the counter." In view of such general awareness, it may not be "resistance to discussing his problems" that
prompts a patient to ask to which school of psychotherapy a
psychiatrist belongs. This resistance may have been a causative
factor twenty-five years ago, when a patient would have had so
much less specific knowledge, and therefore was probably just
trying to delay, stall, or resist. Today, however, the patient
knows something about the various schools, and his inquiry is
likely to be based on preliminary research.

THE PATIENT'S PROBLEMS ARE NOT WHAT DISTINGUISHES HIM; THE ROLE OF DEMORALIZATION

It is said that a psychiatrist once got the chance to speak with
an old Catholic priest who had heard confessions from the great
and small for more than fifty years. What had he observed over
all those years? What is it that people confess? What are the
common sins, the unusual ones, the bizarre ones? Sadly the
priest replied, "It is not their sins that distinguish them. It is
their lack of virtues." In a sense, this aphorism can be adapted
to the person who seeks psychiatric help. Such a person does not
usually come for treatment because he has a unique problem but
because he is demoralized about it. This demoralization (lack of
virtue) is the hallmark of the psychiatric patient. While demoralization or loss of hope can occur transiently in everyday situations, it can also become a person's prevailing emotional framework; at this level demoralization often leads one to seek
psychiatric treatment.

Almost everybody has had the experience of trying to open a
jar and finding that he does not seem to have the strength to do
so. After several unsuccessful attempts, he then hands the jar to
another person who opens it on the first try. "I must have loos-
ened it" is his usual thought, or perhaps he assumes that the
other person is considerably stronger. There is, however,
another possibility: failing the first time, he became slightly
"demoralized," which led to his being unable to exert more

strength the next time, which in turn demoralized him further until, by the time he handed the jar over, his final attempt—although it was the most that he could do—was very weak and more like "going through the motions" than anything else.

The next time someone hands *you* a jar to open after he has failed several times, try a few experiments. Instead of trying to open it yourself, encourage him to try harder. Another alternative might be to take the jar out of his sight and tell him that you are going to do something to the jar which will make it easy to open. Do nothing, and then return it.

Another familiar experience involves swallowing a pill. Once someone has failed to swallow a pill the first time, his subsequent attempts are ineffective because he is discouraged about the possibility of ever being able to get what now seems like an enormous object down his throat. What the person does to help himself, his own personal "strategy," as we shall call it, is often ineffective. Putting the pill on the back of the tongue and tilting the head back, for example, have been shown to interfere with swallowing. After the fifth or sixth time the patient has failed to swallow the pill, he is a rather sorry sight: tilting his head back, sticking his hand in his mouth to position the pill correctly, often gagging as a result, and then puffing out his cheeks and swallowing whole gobs of water only to find that the pill has remained obstinately in his mouth. When there is a serious need to swallow the pill, desperation sets in, and the pill is chewed in spite of its horrible taste and swallowed that way.

Demoralization is a powerful force, as Homer illustrated long ago. In the *Odyssey,* after Odysseus has been gone twenty years, many suitors have come to claim his wife and property. Penelope had said that she would choose a suitor after she completed a tapestry, but each evening she would unravel what she had done the day before. However, this ruse eventually became ineffective as a means of putting off her suitors. Therefore she planned a shooting contest in which the suitor who could string Odysseus's bow and shoot an arrow through the holes in twelve bronze axeheads placed one in front of the other would gain her hand. The contest began and none of the suitors could even string the bow. Then Odysseus, who had just returned disguised as a beggar, rose in rags, strung his own great bow, shot the arrow straight through the axeheads, and began his vengeful slaughter of the suitors. While the reader might assume that none of the suitors were strong enough to string the bow, this is unlikely. Stringing a bow, like opening a jar and swallowing a pill, can be influenced by one's "set" or expectation. More likely, the suitors did not feel that they could string the great bow or measure up to Odysseus, and were demoralized when they made their efforts.

Professional athletes, particularly football players, suffer from the same problem of morale. It is generally acknowledged that they are in top physical condition. Their skills have been well practiced. What makes the difference between winning and losing a game seems to lie in the expectation of the players. One result is that drug abuse has become prevalent in professional football. Amphetamines work the players up to a pitch of aggression and marijuana is used to calm them down (Mandell 1975).

Patients Seek Treatment When They are Demoralized. In the illustrations of the tight jar lid, pill swallowing, Odysseus's bow, and professional football, morale emerges as a vital factor in many tasks. How does this apply to psychiatry? Frank (1973) has documented that patients seek treatment, not when they develop symptoms, but when they are demoralized about them. Three independent lines of investigation have produced findings to support this point: epidemiological studies of psychiatric problems among community residents; outcome studies of psychotherapy which have led to the formulation of the so-called "common feature hypothesis"; and studies of placebos.

In the opinion of professionals, many people in the community have been found to have difficulties that warrant psychiatric diagnosis and treatment. In their elaborate survey of midtown

Manhattan, Srole and his colleagues (1962) found that 80 percent of the residents interviewed manifested some signs of psychopathology; of these, 45 percent were considered by professionals to be moderately or severely disturbed. Yet the rate of diagnosed mental illness in New York City and elsewhere doesn't begin to approach these proportions. The Joint Commission on Mental Illness and Health (1961) estimated that only 14 percent of those with psychiatric difficulties actually sought help from clergymen, physicians, social agencies, or mental health professionals. One may assume that a distinguishing characteristic of this 14 percent is that they are despairing, demoralized, and no longer think they will get better or survive with their problems.

At the individual level, an observer may note that loss of hope rather than symptom onset is usually the factor that leads to help-seeking efforts. For example, a young man has a bout with impotence. He does not seek help immediately, despite his distress, because he hopes that it will go away or that he will figure out some way to deal with it. He can still function sexually with an old girl friend, although not with new ones. He doesn't feel discouraged about his problem. However, a series of events eventually make him lose hope about finding a solution. A priest whom he has known for many years is appalled by his sexual mores and tells him that he has been using his penis "like a sword," and a college English professor of dubious sexual preference suggests that he may be a latent homosexual. He finally becomes impotent with his old girl friend, is thoroughly discouraged (demoralized), and seeks psychiatric help. (He has had my name for approximately two years.) The first goal with such a patient is to increase his morale, to get his hopes up; otherwise he will follow advice with the same lack of conviction, effort, or attention to the task that occurred in our examples of opening a bottle and swallowing a pill.

The second line of investigation suggesting that patients seek therapy because of demoralization rather than symptom onset has led to the formulation of the "common feature hypothesis," based on outcome research in psychotherapy. As both its advocates and detractors have observed, widely disparate varieties of psychotherapy yield more or less equivalent rates of improvement. Furthermore, experienced senior clinicians practicing different strategies resemble each other more in their behavior and effectiveness than they do inexperienced therapists sharing their therapeutic persuasion. Frank (1973) has concluded from such findings that the features common to all forms of psychotherapy contribute to their effectiveness far more significantly than any specific individual aspect. Thus, while a Jungian might analyze a dream with the technique of "active imagination" and a behavior therapist might not even discuss the dream at all, both approaches achieve comparable rates of success because they, in common with all other effective methods of psychotherapy, give the patient hope.

The common feature hypothesis gains considerable support from anthropological investigations. Torrey (1973) has reviewed psychic healing among witch doctors and psychiatrists and concluded: "Psychiatric therapies are very similar all over the world and are relatively independent of the level of technology, the education of the therapists, or the theories of causation. Psychiatry is just as scientific—or prescientific—in rural Nigeria or the mountains of Mexico as it is in New York or San Francisco" (Torrey 1973, p. 11). My own experience with Puerto Rican spiritualists also supports the common feature hypothesis. A competent spiritualist is just as capable of gaining control of a patient's expectations, of getting him to expect to benefit from the experience, as a competent psychiatrist. Both bolster the patient's morale.

The third source of support for the observation that morale is of utmost importance derives from studies of the "placebo effect." For years it has been observed that medicine without pharmacological value apparently can induce medical or psychiatric improvement, and it has been a puzzle for physicians who have not considered the role of the patient's expectations. Were it a limited observation, an occasional occurrence, the puzzle might be intriguing but unimportant. However, before the twentieth century placebos were virtually all that medicine had to offer sick patients, apart from the risks of surgery. More recently, studies have suggested that somewhere between one-third and two-fifths of all prescriptions written in the United States make no pharmacological contribution but help the patient as placebos (Shapiro 1960). As Dubois noted, "although placebos are scarcely mentioned in the literature, they are administered more than any other group of drugs. . . . Although few doctors admit that they give placebos, there is a placebo ingredient in practically every prescription" (quoted in Shapiro 1960, p. 121). It is the placebo effect that gives the patient hope, whether or not this was the physician's intention. I have spoken to patients who felt much better after "their treatment," which turned out to be a routine chest X ray. Paracelsus wrote 400 years ago:

Faith in the gods or in the saints cures one, faith in little pills another, hypnotic suggestion a third, faith in a plain common doctor a fourth. . . . Faith in us, faith in our drugs and methods, is the great stock in trade of the profession . . . while we doctors often overlook or are ignorant of our own faith-cures, we are just a wee bit too sensitive about those performed outside our ranks (quoted in Shapiro 1960, p. 117).

The problem with the term "placebo" is that it somehow makes the therapist feel cheap—he is "pleasing the patient." There is also an emphasis, which the therapist dislikes, on the administration of a medicine. It would be better to coin a word that means "I give hope" instead of "I please," as "placebo" suggests. There is such a word in Greek, *elpisophoron*, meaning an inanimate object that is the "bearer of hope." The effect of increasing a patient's hope is not something that we wish to eliminate from our therapy, however much we may otherwise lament the use of "sugar pills."

Lack of Effort in Treatment. One of the major consequences of demoralization, and a common source of therapeutic
failure, is insufficient effort on the part of the patient. Such a
patient halfheartedly follows instructions, merely "goes through
the motions," or is "overly cooperative." He does not take the
initiative or add anything personal to the treatment plan. Since
he is in a position to know more about what is happening in any
specific transaction outside of the therapist's office, it is essential
that he add his own judgment to any suggestions that are made,
in addition to expending considerable effort. For example, a
patient who is obese can dutifully seek help without really
believing that anything can be done for him. He might be given
a directive or task, perhaps to keep an exact record of everything he eats, but he will do so in a desultory way, bringing in to
the next session a small piece of wrinkled paper with some scrib-
bling on it. Clearly such a patient is not making sufficient effort.

Psychiatric commentators often associate lack of effort with
lack of motivation, or with the underlying motivation to sabo-
tage the therapy and an unconscious effort to remain ill. It is
also possible that a lack of effort is associated with demoralization, as I have discussed. A third explanation, focusing on cogni-
tion rather than affect, as in the concept of demoralization, concerns the individual's evaluation of his own powers of influence.
Some patients, even if they are eager to change, may not try
hard because they don't think their actions will have an impact
on events. In contrast to the sense of *hopelessness* implied in
demoralization, where the patient feels things won't ever change
for the better, some people experience a sense of *helplessness*
whereby change, though possible, is not under their influence.

This concept has been formulated by Rotter (1954) in terms
of locus of control. If a person feels he has influence over the
events that happen to him, he is said to have an "internal" locus
of control, while those who believe that their lives are controlled
by chance, fate, or powerful others are said to have an "external" locus of control. Locus of control does not refer to motiva-

tion. Many people in our society would like to improve their conditions but realistically they have low expectations for success. For example, most poor people make little effort to improve their financial position. There is a critical relationship between *can* and *try*: a person does not try if he does not believe that he can succeed.

Because "internals" are more prone than "externals" to try to shape events, they are more likely to participate actively in a treatment plan suggested by a psychotherapist. A patient with an internal locus of control will accept a proposed task as something he can do himself to improve his condition; the therapist is seen as a facilitator who "helps him to help himself." Further, the "internal" is likely to accept gradual improvement if it is related to what he himself does, and is more willing to deal with a complex set of circumstances. In contrast, the patient with an external locus of control is likely to expect a "wonder session," in which the therapist's actions are entirely responsible for whatever change occurs. For such a patient, therapeutic prescriptions must entail simple, passive acts which allow the outside force, the therapist, to cure him.

Locus of control, as distinct from demoralization, has been measured by questionnaire and has lent itself to systematic study. Demoralization, on the other hand, is intuitively understood by coaches, military commanders, and teachers. That which a strategic psychotherapist can do to shift the locus of control from external to internal or to increase morale clearly improves the prognosis.

THE PATIENT IS NOT SURE WHAT IS THE MATTER

It is generally believed that people get sick, go to a doctor, follow his prescriptions, and then recover; this seems to be a self-evident sequence of events. However, people do not immediately "get sick." The notion that "I am sick" is a conclusion a person reaches after considering several other possibilities, some of which may be quite erroneous. For example, a physician ordered installation of a burglar alarm system in his house. The electrician sent to do the job noticed that the doctor wanted an inordinate number of components. A few days after installation was completed, the physician died of a heart ailment. Probably he had a sense of being uneasy, not being at ease, or "dis-ease." However, in spite of his medical training he attributed the cause to a concern about external danger shared by many of his fellow New Yorkers, rather than to his unidentified heart condition. In a sense he had a premonition that something was going to happen. He was unfortunately correct, but the nature of the problem had been incorrectly diagnosed.

People seldom go to a doctor as soon as they decide that they are or might be sick. They try various home remedies, wait and see, or talk to the druggist and the bartender. In some instances no feasible action can be undertaken at the earliest stages of an evolving disorder, as in the case of muscular dystrophy. But in many other cases prompt intervention can make a large difference. In psychiatry it is not uncommon for a patient to contact a psychiatrist a year or more after he has gotten the psychiatrist's name, and it is likely that the name was obtained a while after he began to suffer from some difficulty.

Even when people conclude that they should visit a physician, they are not necessarily sick, nor do they always have a clear idea of what is bothering them. For example, it is commonly said that 60 percent of those who consult general practitioners are not sick (Richardson 1945). When a former mayor of New York established "little city halls" in health stations and clinics, where one could get administrative or legal help, sometimes as many as 60 percent of the patients who first presented themselves at the clinic were sent on to these facilities. How could this be?

When someone is upset or faced with a stressful situation, there are very few people to whom to go for advice, consolation, administrative assistance, or just conversation. For many, stress is associated in some fashion with a new, uncomfortable bodily feeling. Therefore it seems natural to visit one's doctor. At this point in time there is still an unorganized quality to the problem. The patient is not sure what is the matter, and neither is the doctor. If the patient were to have gone somewhere else, let us say to a clergyman, there would still be a vague, unorganized aspect to the problem, but the physical, bodily aspects would probably be ignored or deemphasized.

Balint (1957) met with a group of general practitioners in London and together they discussed the process by which this amorphous state of conflict, stress, or discomfort sometimes became organized into a distinct illness. In examining their experiences, they noticed that before doctor and patient settled on one diagnostic condition, there was a period of *negotiation* in which the patient (or the doctor) proposed various possible alternatives until an agreement could be reached between them. Psychiatric referral is one such possibility.

The concept of a vague or unorganized beginning and a negotiation process is somewhat difficult to accept for the doctor who is not on the "front lines." A specialist is accustomed to receiving referrals from other physicians or consultants who have already negotiated a problem with the patient. At other times, family members negotiate with the patient. However, those who have had experience in emergency rooms or hospital admitting offices before becoming specialists usually remember a few outstanding cases in which the diagnosis was spectacularly wrong. I have seen patients sent to surgery for hernias who, in fact, have had scrotal edema from heart failure. Recently I saw a bright, observant woman who complained of a bewildering array of about fifteen symptoms, ranging from headache to funny feelings just above the knee and the feeling that she was about to have a bowel movement. She had gonorrhea, but did not know it then. By the time she returned a few days later, after having been seen in the gynecological clinic, her complaints had been narrowed down, "negotiated," to vaginal discharge (which she did not originally complain of spontaneously because she thought that she always had a slight discharge) and low abdominal pains. It is not unusual for a patient to present his complaints using various types of imagery, sometimes personal ("butterflies in the stomach"), until the negotiation process narrows their focus and restricts the symptoms to a few consenually acceptable terms. I once saw an elderly man who spoke English badly admitted to a psychiatric ward as paranoid for complaining about being killed when, in fact, he was complaining about "killing pains" in his chest. He was having a heart attack. The "they" which were killing him turned out to be his description of his pains.

I am not telling stories about incompetent diagnoses to show how bad the medical profession is. The point of mentioning these egregious errors is to illustrate how difficult it is to narrow down and construct (with the patient's help) a consensually accepted set of symptoms, and thereby arrive at a diagnosis. Although one might think that the doctor offers the most input into such a decision, studies using "pseudopatients" (Rosenhan 1973) suggest that the patient has quite a lot to say about his diagnosis. A pseudopatient is a perfectly healthy or sane individual who is sent to assess the physician's capacities. Rosenhan's studies described how he and seven other normal people gained admission to a number of reputable psychiatric hospitals solely by coming to the admissions office with the complaint that they had heard voices. They answered all other questions with information from their own lives.

There are occasions when an impasse is reached in the negotiation process and patient and doctor cannot agree upon the nature of the problem. I believe that this inability to negotiate an illness is the matrix from which the diagnosis of conversion hysteria can develop (Rabkin 1964). I would classify such a patient—one who has been "worked up" extensively and then referred to a psychotherapist—as one with whom the therapist is at a distinct disadvantage, because the patient will have had several months of training in viewing himself as medically ill.

If at the outset the patient and the doctor are both not sure what the problem is, there is an opportunity to shape the amorphous dough of discomfort in ways that will be most helpful to the patient. By selecting our cookie cutters with the utmost care, we can stamp out of that dough certain forms that have a strategic advantage to the patient and the therapy. Notably, we can pinpoint specific behavioral problems.

THE PATIENT HAS ATTEMPTED A STRATEGY AND IT HAS FAILED

Opening a jar and swallowing a pill exemplify problems in the initial phases of strategic therapy in another fashion besides illustrating demoralization. In both instances the subject had a "strategy." In the case of difficult pill swallowing the head tilting and placement of the pill on the back of the tongue are commonsense strategies which many people try. They never work. What is needed is an uncommonsense strategy. On a recent vacation with my six-year-old son I found he was having difficulty swallowing a pill with commonsense strategies; I took the pill and told him that I was going to make it even bigger, so big that it wouldn't even fit in his mouth. He found this amusing and swallowed a pill for the first time in his life without further difficulty. Prior to this I imagine his attention had been on two things: that I would be angry at him for not swallowing the pill, and the sensation of the pill in his mouth. Both of these preoccupations made it difficult for him to swallow the pill. My exaggeration of the size of the pill might have made it seem much smaller when he put it in his mouth. I am not recommending this strategy as a solution to all pill-swallowing difficulties; it is merely an illustration of an uncommonsense strategy.

Most people seek psychiatric help after commonsense efforts to resolve their troubles have failed. It is essential to know about these previous efforts. In the simplest case the strategy is an exhortation to change. For example, a sad or depressed person might be told to cheer up and that things are not as bad as he thinks, or a child with a habit problem (a tic, for example) might be admonished to stop, frightened, or punished. When

such approaches work—and at times they do—there is no need
for a psychiatrist. When patients can obtain information about
such problems from books or lectures, there is no need for a
psychiatrist. Psychiatric help is, therefore, sought after there has
already been a failure. Accompanying this failure is demoralization.

In community psychiatry it is assumed that local residents
should be helped by various members of their everyday environment, such as schoolteachers, guidance counselors, the druggist,
bartender, and grocer's wife. It is further assumed that when
such help is insufficient, the role of the community mental health
worker is to back up these indigenous helpers rather than deal
immediately with the problem himself. However, indigenous
helpers are likely to suggest commonsense solutions, and when
these fail it is seldom helpful to try more of the same. Instead,
the types of strategy that must be suggested are uncommonsense
types. Haley (1973a) entitled his book about Erickson *Uncommon Therapy,* in order to emphasize this point. Because uncommonsense strategies are used in the psychiatric clinic, there is a
discontinuity between community and clinic which has led me to
be more pessimistic than most commentators about the possibility of psychiatrists backing up various indigenous helpers. Psychotherapists, from a lack of experience, may not know what to
do with simple problems, and the community does not know
what to do with more complex ones that have failed to respond
to common sense.

When someone reaches a psychiatrist before exhausting commonsense strategies, that is, before seeking advice from commu-
nity-based helpers, the proper recommendation is for him to
return to such helpers and such advice. He should not be
inducted into patienthood. It is not appropriate to attempt a
strategic or uncommonsense approach until other approaches
have failed.

A patient with headaches came to see me (referred by a neurologist), very upset about the fact that she was having an affair

with her interior decorator. I asked her with whom she usually talked over her problems. She said that she had a best friend but couldn't think of burdening her with such a problem. We agreed that before she obtained any advice from me she would try speaking to her best friend. I heard nothing from the patient for several weeks. She then told me that she had been greatly relieved by speaking to her friend, who gave her some very fine advice which worked. She no longer complained about headaches.

It is also possible to identify situations in which the commonsense approaches have not taken place, as in the mourning process. A patient came to see me depressed about the death of her son, which had occurred more than a year before. She reported, in the course of some other discussion, that his room was intact: his eyeglasses were still where he left them on his desk, his clothes were still in the closet. I asked her to call a close relative to come and get rid of his belongings. I then encouraged the patient to take some action on her plan to create a memorial to him. In this case the usual help that someone in mourning obtains from close relatives, helping to get rid of the possessions of the deceased, had not taken place. This probably contributed to the length of the mourning that had been going on. (The patient improved after the relative came and did her job.)

When commonsense strategies do not help, unusual measures must be attempted. The child with tics who does not improve with commonsense measures might be told to practice his tics in front of a mirror. A depressed person might be told to try to become even more depressed. When a depressed patient is told that, given his terrible circumstances, one would expect him to be much more depressed than he already is, such a prescription or strategy operates not on the depression, but on the *context*. In most cases common sense works; however, when it does not, it can make a depressed person even more depressed, perhaps by invalidating the sad feelings or making the patient feel even more of a failure. At this point what must be changed is the approach. Almost any change would be better than repeating a strategy that is not working or that is making a patient worse.

The fact that patients have usually tried a strategy, and that a therapist usually must devote most of his time to changing that strategy, suggests that it is essential to know what a patient has attempted up to the moment of being seen. Broadly speaking, such strategies can be classified as "doing something by doing nothing" (i.e., the patient has tried to ignore his problem) or as "more of the same" (the patient is repeating over and over again an ineffective problem-solving attempt [Watzlawick, Weakland, and Fisch 1974]). If the patient is doing nothing, it might be a good idea to suggest that he work out a specific way of dealing with his problem. On the other hand, if he is doing more of the same any change might be in order, sometimes even doing nothing.

Frequently the strategy of doing something by doing nothing, or benign neglect, is helpful. For example, stuttering is a transient speech disorder of many children. If it is neglected it frequently ceases. However, there are times when this strategy should be changed. I recently saw a patient who had tension headaches for many years, and who reported that she had tried to do absolutely nothing about them. In this case it was time to try something, and one could suggest that the prognosis would be favorable since there had been no failures.

More of the same, or persistence, is frequently a successful strategy. However, in the example of opening a jar we saw a more-of-the-same strategy when it did not work. There are instances when people make the same mistake repeatedly; their need is to change strategies. The official policy toward drug addiction is to attempt to keep dangerous or narcotic drugs out of the country. In recent months there have been some slight suggestions that the government may yet conclude, after fifty years of trying the same strategy, that there should be a change. Any alternative would be better than another ineffective fifty years of more of the same.

Finally, there is the strategy of the "total push," or doing everything that is possible. This, too, is very successful at times. However, we frequently see people in panic situations who are doing too much, each thing superficially. They claim to have "tried everything" only to find that nothing works. Usually they have not given any one approach sufficient time. I have seen patients who have consulted so many doctors and obtained so much, often conflicting, advice that they run around without knowing where they are heading. This is the "chronic hurry syndrome." For them to get somewhere quicker, paradoxically, they have to slow down.

THE PATIENT IS NOT PREPARED FOR LONG-TERM THERAPY

While the labels "long-term" and "short-term" appear to refer only to treatment duration, characteristically they reflect treatment strategy and philosophy as well. Long-term therapy is almost invariably based on a psychoanalytic model and generally entails several visits a week for periods ranging from one year to five or more. During the 1940s and 1950s long-term treatment was usually regarded by most professionals and psychiatrists in training as the treatment of choice for those with the requisite assets (moral, intellectual, and financial). Psychiatrists at the beginning of their training were given short-term treatment assignments, while more experienced residents saw patients in long-term treatment.

In the last fifteen years, in conjunction with the growth of community psychiatry, increasing attention and enthusiasm have been devoted to alternate treatment methods. Views and values, especially among younger therapists, have now evolved to the point where short-term therapy is seen as a respectable alternative treatment program. Where once the less-skilled therapist and more poorly endowed patient were relegated to the lesser status of weekly sessions covering months instead of years, today it is often the converse: training in long-term therapy precedes brief therapy in residency programs, and many competent, artic-

ulate patients are seen for abbreviated time intervals and cir-
cumscribed problems. Whereas once long-term therapy was seen
as more sophisticated and harder to master, the reverse is now
often the case.

It is necessary to add that the model of private practice developed in the United States rewards long-term therapy. For example, Aldrich remarks:

> The pattern of private psychotherapeutic practice encourages
> pessimism. A resident who takes the plunge into private practice is
> understandably apprehensive. After so many years of training, his
> financial needs are considerable and his confidence about his ability
> to keep his treatment hours filled may be limited. As he accumulates
> patients, however, his confidence increases and his apprehension
> diminishes. His patients give him security, and he is predisposed to
> keep them with him. Training which emphasizes the value of long-
> term treatment, which has categorized the "best" treatment cases as
> "long-term" even before his first interview, which stresses the im-
> portance of resolution of all the patient's conflicts before letting
> him go on his own, and which encourages the interpretation of
> early improvement as a "flight into health," to be explored and in
> effect broken down—training with this pessimistic flavor supports
> his bias towards long-term treatment (Aldrich 1968, p. 591).

Aldrich notes that patients chosen for long-term therapy are
supposed to have strong egos, according to the theory of long-
term therapy. He adds that they must also have strong egos to
survive the pessimism and dependency inherent in the long-term
process.

In the United States since World War II, when psychotherapy
first became widely available to the general public, the typical
therapeutic method offered in both private and clinic practice
was based on a psychoanalytic model and usually lasted a year
or more. Since there were far more prospective patients than
therapists could see, some selection process was inevitable.
Usually patients were chosen on the basis of the "suitability
model" (Lazare et al. 1972): treatment was offered to those
patients who were seen as suited to the treatment. Such patients

have been referred to as "YAVIS": Young, Attractive, Verbal, Intelligent, and Successful. They qualified for prolonged treatment by the very fact that they were not seriously impaired to begin with, and were demonstrably competent in their daily lives.

In the past several years a number of investigators have found that most prospective psychiatric patients, regardless of social class or symptomatology, expected therapy to require five to ten sessions (Garfield 1971; Levitt 1966). As Lorion (1974) has noted, these expected durations do not differ materially from actual national average durations where median has been reported by numerous independent observers to be five to six sessions.

Studies of single-session psychotherapy indicate that this is neither a rare nor necessarily ineffective occurrence. A study done at the Kaiser Foundation Health Plan of Southern California found that in 1969, 27 percent of the psychiatric patients seen only had a single interview (Reed, Myers, and Scheidemandel 1972). Spoerl (1975), in his own mental health clinic which functions as part of a private prepaid nonprofit health maintenance organization, found that 39 percent of the 6,780 patients who were seen in 1972 made only one visit to the clinic. Obviously some of these patients were "dropouts" from psychotherapy who for one reason or another did not maintain contact. However, Spoerl has collected a significant series of cases in which the patient was helped sufficiently in the first interview that there was no need for a second.

One of Spoerl's cases is of a middle-aged man who consulted him about a long-lasting depressive state, the onset of which he dated to the accidental death of his wife. While cleaning his hunting rifle in one room, the weapon discharged and the bullet penetrated a wall of the adjoining bedroom, killing his wife. His wife was dedicated to her nursing career, and Spoerl recommended that the patient establish a memorial scholarship for financially needy nursing students. An appointment was set up with the assistant dean of the local nursing school. In a follow-up two weeks later the patient was visibly less depressed, and no longer complained that his life held no meaning for him.

In light of these recent observations about patient expectations and the possibilities of effective change through brief psychotherapy, various therapists have suggested that patients be given some choice regarding treatment plans. One such approach, developed by Lazare and his colleagues (1972), is called the "customer approach to patienthood." Faced with training first-year residents in a walk-in clinic of a general hospital, they hit upon the idea of having the residents inquire about the patient's request rather than conduct an interview to determine the patient's suitability. Lazare and his group have evolved a seventy-five-item questionnaire which classifies requests into fifteen largely independent categories. All but one of these categories can be thought of as a request for short-term therapy.

It is instructive to examine the one request that is for long-term therapy. Lazare and his colleagues (1972) describe such patients as coming for therapy to gain insight. These patients believe that an understanding of current and past problems is an essential part of the treatment. In contrast to other patients, who request that the psychiatrist help them to put things into perspective, sort out various psychological problems, or otherwise intervene rather briefly, this type of patient expects long-term therapy and usually has friends or relatives whom he would describe as being "in therapy." Although Lazare does not suggest it, it appears that such a patient has been educated to seek such treatment.

I am not in a position to report personally on the atmosphere among intellectual circles during the heyday of insight-oriented approaches. However, Eysenck states that "The average upper-middle-class inhabitant of New York, Boston, Los Angeles, or Kansas City would be considered as much out of things if he were unable to talk about his 'psychoanalyst' as would his Parisian counterpart who could not boast a mistress" (Eysenck

1957, p. 27). If anything like this atmosphere held sway in upper-middle-class circles, one could see why people sought insight-oriented psychotherapy rather than short-term, problem-oriented therapy. Whether the *Zeitgeist* is responsible for producing such patients is less significant than the fact that they were never numerous.

I have seen several patients who had a rather specific and limited problem but, because they were well educated, presented themselves as seeking insight in order to improve their general psychological development. It was as if they knew enough to have supposed (*correctly*) that they would be judged by the average therapist based on their suitability for long-term therapy. For example, a rather insecure woman has finally left her ineffective boyfriend and, from Lazare's point of view, is seeking advice and support. Her family is of no help to her. Rather than state this at the outset, she presents the therapist with a general desire to improve herself.

Not only is the typical patient expecting short-term therapy, but he is not in a position to extend the time he has allotted for it. As with each of the other aspects in our description of the patient, this determines certain goals of strategic therapy. We must be able to work within the allotted time.

Strategic psychotherapy is tailored to each patient's specific problems and capacities, in contrast to psychoanalysis, for example, where universal problems such as the Oedipus complex are assumed and treated. It is therefore particularly helpful in planning strategies to understand the patient's expectations about therapy, his concepts regarding the locus of control, the extent of his demoralization, and his past efforts to define and solve his problem. The therapist can then hope to take advantage of some of these characteristics in treatment, and prevent others from interfering with his strategies.

CHAPTER 2

Healing Fictions:

The Therapist's Initial

Contribution to Treatment

WHEN HE SEEKS HELP, the psychiatric patient is usually unsure of himself, the nature of his problem, and his expectations of psychotherapy. The therapist is immediately cast in a role in which he must offer the patient hope, negotiate about and define the problem to be addressed in treatment, and convince the patient of his power to be helpful. As I have indicated, I regard these preliminary tasks as crucial to a successful therapeutic outcome. In this chapter I shall discuss methods for achieving them and some reasons for their importance.

"Healing fictions" is the term Jung used to describe his observation that patients seemed to improve when he could make something meaningful out of their problems with his rather imaginative theories, although etiological factors had not been changed. In this Jungian sense the entire opening phase of strategic psychotherapy requires us, as authors of the diagnosis and prognosis, to distinguish between the mythical (nonexistent) and the mythic (powerful), between bureaucratic requirements and genuinely therapeutic ritual.

I shall first describe the practical details of greeting a new patient. Next I shall consider the therapist's posture at the outset regarding the patient's initial remarks, and some methods for shaping the patient's complaint so that it becomes a suitable, soluble therapeutic problem within reasonable limits. I then touch upon the issue of "briefing" the patient about what to expect in the course of his work in psychotherapy, and "debriefing" him regarding any previous psychotherapy experiences. Because biographical study, or the "strategy of reminiscence," is so often routinely begun in dynamic psychotherapy, I end this chapter by shifting to a discussion of the use of biographical material in strategic and dynamic therapy, and the closely associated concept of emotional catharsis which is supposed to follow autobiographical discoveries.

THE INITIAL CONTACT

My office, like most, consists of a waiting room and a consultation room. The patient enters an empty waiting room; if he has never visited a psychiatrist before, he may wonder whether he is at the right place. If I can, I try to excuse myself from what I am doing to greet a new patient briefly if I suspect that he may be worried about this. Some patients accustomed to crowded waiting rooms and long delays assume that the physician must be unpopular if his waiting room is empty. Freud had such an experience. The patient, according to Freud, expressed this attitude by not shutting the door behind him. Freud reportedly dealt with this by a curt reminder.

I have noticed that most patients who feel at least slightly at home make some small talk in the waiting room. It seems helpful to allow or actually encourage this to occur, although other therapists might regard this as a challenge to their authority and status. For example, I was once asked to view a videotape in which a carpenter and his family came for therapy. In the waiting room the carpenter noticed that there was some unfinished carpentry. He made a few somewhat technical remarks about it in a friendly manner, and the therapist cut him off. I would prefer to allow the carpenter to teach me something about his field, since the tables are going to be reversed when we enter the consultation room. I sometimes think of this preliminary conversation as the preoperative medication.

In the consultation room I gather the briefest "vital statistics," which include name, address, telephone numbers, age, profession and occupation (so that I can get some idea of social class), previous therapeutic experiences, and medical status (last physical examination). I then let the patient talk about whatever he wishes. If the case is one in which a natural group (couple or family) is the "patient" I begin by suggesting that the group members talk among *themselves* about what they think is the problem. I do not want one member to tell me about the problem, but insist that they speak to each other while I watch as well as listen. In that way I may be able to witness something they would not have told me or observed themselves.

I do not begin by taking a history. I have questions in my own mind about the historical development of the problem as well as the biography of the patient, but to begin by taking a standard psychiatric history implies certain assumptions which are transmitted to the patient. For example, Kolb writes that in the interview:

One wishes to learn whether the patient was a wanted or unwanted child and what expectations the parents might have held for his sex and future development. . . . The nature of the birth itself and the mother's reaction to it often determine mothering attitudes for long periods thereafter and are worthy of discussion.

An account should be obtained of the ages at which sitting, walking, talking, and bowel and bladder control took place . . . (Kolb 1973, p. 153).

I believe that if the therapist wants to know the patient's earliest memory, the implication is that the problem is developmental and stems from those times. This is the classic route into long-term self-study and therapy: The patient comes with a current problem about which he is demoralized and wants to talk about it. The therapist selectively ignores it while inquiring about seemingly irrelevant details of his childhood. On the positive side we can say that the confusion created by this approach gives the therapist certain leverage. If he should ever, as an aside, offer some advice for the current problem, the patient will grasp for it eagerly after being distracted by these unexpected historical inquiries. The nature and role of biographic material is discussed at length in the second half of this chapter.

While the patient discusses what he wants, or the group members talk among themselves about the problem, I glance at a clipboard on which I have an outline of material to be covered (see appendix A). As the process unfolds I try to make sure that each item is touched on in the ensuing discussion. I do not necessarily follow the exact order, but use the outline to make sure that every step has been covered at some time during the session or sessions devoted to the opening. In most instances many of the points will have been covered spontaneously. However, when a particular item is missing, it is necessary to be aware of it. The most common error of the beginning therapist is to rush into a midgame strategy or tactic, perhaps because the therapist is anxious to exercise his newly developed skills. Ironically, his therapeutic success probably depends almost completely on the patient's expectations, and hence on issues related to the ensuing material.

DEFINING THE COMPLAINT, THE GOAL, AND THE REQUEST

The patient offers a variety of problems and options, which he and the therapist define further. For example, in a general medical clinic I have heard a patient way, "I have a lot of trouble with my husband and a backache." While there are some patients like this one, who present clear options between backaches and difficult husbands, there are others who present particularly vague complaints. Such patients complain that "I do not know who I am," "I cannot communicate," "I have an inferiority complex," and so on. It is necessary under these circumstances to attempt to pinpoint a problem. In fact, certain therapists have assumed that these patients are suffering more from the consequences of approaching problems with such vagueness than from anything else. They are committed to considerations that are so general, vague, grandiose, and sometimes verbose that they are unable to adapt successfully to the specifics of life.

Sometimes such patients cannot seem to begin defining a problem. The therapist may choose to be more general than the patient in order to force him to attempt the task of defining a manageable problem. For example, Weakland and colleagues report the following case:

A student who was already in his mid-20's and was still being supported by a working mother told us he was studying "philosophical anthropology" in order to bring the light of India and China to bear on the West. He also, however, mentioned some interest in attending a well-known school of Indian music. It was then pointed out to him that this represented a rather limited aim compared to his concern to unite the spirituality of India with the practical communism of China and use both to reconstruct Western society. He then said that, since he was not doing well in his studies and was short of money, if he could secure a scholarship and really learn Indian music, this would be quite enough accomplishment for the present (Weakland et al. 1974, p. 154).

When a patient attempts to define a complaint, he usually has some sort of a goal in mind. For example, a depressed patient can wish "to feel better," "to feel happy," or "to feel well enough to go back to work." It is generally better to try to use a delimited goal such as last named. "To feel better" is too vague, while "to feel happy" is too extreme. As this illustrates, it is best to define a goal in behavioral terms. Weakland and colleagues also suggest that one "think small": "Our usual inquiry is something like 'at a minimum, what [change in] behavior would indicate to you that a definite step forward has been made on your problem?" (Weakland et al. 1974, p. 154). This sort of an inquiry negotiates for the smallest possible change rather than cure.

Under circumstances when patients present goals that are small and behavioral, the negotiation process is minimized. Early referral to a psychiatrist from a medical colleague is the most common source of such patients. While late referral from a medical colleague is a common source of conversion reactions, early referral produces some of the most easily treated cases. This is because medical doctors generally attempt to negotiate the same type of complaint and goal as do strategic psychotherapists. There is considerable compatibility between the two approaches. This is not an endorsement of the so-called "medical model" of therapy, but is rather a statement about the clinical approach. The medical model emphasizes organic causes and treatments, whereas the clinical approach involves negotiating a workable goal.

The concept of a specified goal, a particular problem to be dealt with, cannot be arrived at from certain psychoanalytic points of view. For example, in what purports to be a "complete guide to therapy" for the layman the following statement appears:

Neurotic functioning consists of a set of imbalances . . . such that unconscious spheres take destructive control. There are no foreign bodies here, nothing that exists in isolation from anything else, or that can be removed, like a splinter or a bacillus. More, there is no real standard of health that can be appealed to the way a doctor can, for example, measure the progress of a healing fracture by comparing it to the natural form of the bone. For the body lives within nature, which has its own harmonies; but the self lives between nature and history, two spheres that, as you know, often don't get on too well with each other. We cannot therefore conceive of the health of the individual apart from that of the social whole in which he is imbedded—and . . . there is as yet no therapy that takes more than faltering steps down this path (Kovel 1976, p. 125).

As with patients who define their problems vaguely and broadly, once a therapist adopts this attitude toward his job he must enter into a long-term, total moral correction of the patient rather than a short-term, problem-oriented therapy. Rieff (1959) has emphasized the moralistic quality of this sort of thinking. I wish to emphasize its clinical effects—longer and longer treatment durations.

For brief therapy, it is important that the patient and the therapist obtain the clearest possible statement of a goal which will serve to indicate when they have achieved their aim. For example, if a child is doing badly in school, what is the criterion of success? You do not want to require the child to get all A's, but there is a need to establish some standard toward which he can strive. On the other hand, sometimes it is helpful to be very concrete. When is someone over a dog phobia? If one is concrete and says, "When you allow a dog to lick your hand, the dog phobia will be over," it helps the patient to put an end to his worries. Setting a clear goal is instrumental in terminating therapy as well as in getting started.

As mentioned in the previous chapter, Lazare and his colleagues (1972) have suggested that attention be paid to the patient's idea of what should be done for him, in addition to his complaint and a goal. Some care must be taken in obtaining what they call "the request," since a brisk "What do you want?" will sound as if the therapist is not interested. In addition, patients are sometimes shy about discussing their hopes. With care ("What is it that you hoped I could do for you?") and after hearing the patient out, Lazare has found that requests fall into fifteen largely independent categories: administrative, advice, clarification, community triage (information about community resources), confession, control, limit setting, medical, psychological expertise, psychotherapy, social intervention, reality contact, succorance, ventilation, and none (e.g., patients who are brought involuntarily.)

Lazare reports that the request is often simpler than the demand a therapist puts upon himself. In one case, the complaint of a bothersome psychotic woman concerning "noise pollution" was turned into a sensible and soluble problem. Her rambling, circuitous, and frustrating style of being interviewed changed completely when she was asked what it was she hoped. She said simply that she wanted stronger medication. To the surprise of the interviewer, it was discovered that chlordiazepoxide hydrochloride (Librium) was all that she had been given.

The final result of the negotiation process is that the patient defines a *complaint* ("I am depressed"), pinpoints a *goal* ("I would like to feel well enough to return to work"), and develops a *request* ("Tell my family to stop criticizing me"). A depressed patient might have a host of vague complaints, some of which might be idiosyncratic or expressed in personal imagery. These are shaped into consensually valid terms like "depression." His goal might similarly be vague or unrealistic; this, too, is shaped by the negotiation. I have already mentioned that "cure" is often an unrealistic goal. It is better to think small. The same applies to the request. While a patient initially might want the psychotherapist to be a doctor and give him medication, this request might be tactfully shaped into other therapeutic modalities.

ESTABLISHING A DIAGNOSIS

The negotiation proceeds toward a diagnosis, prognosis, explanation, and something that I have called "the limiting move."

Torrey (1973) has pointed out that one of the helpful things done by both therapists and witch doctors is to *name* the disease or the offending agent. It is exceedingly unhelpful, for example, to interview a child, have him take a battery of psychological tests, and then present the worried parents with a lukewarm dynamic statement like "Jimmy has a little trouble communicating." What the parents want, among other things, is a name. There are parents who are more content with a term like "schizophrenia"—which has such dire connotations to a psychiatrist —than the ambiguity in the above remark.

It is helpful to give patients a definite name for what is troubling them and, if possible, mention that it is not rare and that the therapist has seen many cases like it before. The name need not be from the American Psychiatric Association's diagnostic manual. In fact, it would be better to use ordinary language to describe the problem. However, one must be specific. For example, one can say that the patient is suffering from being "unassertive."

After giving the patient a name for his problem, it is necessary to give him a *brief* explanation so that he can make some sense out of it. One of the possible ways of giving an explanation for a condition is to link it to a growth crisis or transition in his life. Entering school, getting married, and having children are all periods of stress (although our culture tends to romanticize these events); it is possible to use the stress as the foundation of an explanation.

It is helpful if, after naming and explaining the condition, the therapist can offer assurances that there are strategies for dealing with the problem, that he is confident of being able to help (but not cure—one cannot ethically or legally promise cure), and that he has had success with previous patients.

After the patient and the therapist have established a soluble problem which the patient feels requires the therapist's help to resolve, the therapist should deliberately limit the scope of therapeutic inquiry. That is, he should indicate that the patient is competent in other areas of functioning apart from the particular problem, saying in effect: "When this problem is solved your future looks good."

It is helpful in all therapy to indicate what is *not* a problem. For example, it is often important in general medical practice, no matter what reason a patient comes to see you, to indicate that the patient does not have cancer. In psychiatry low intelligence, homosexuality, and schizophrenia rank high as worries of which patients or their relatives must be disabused. It might be noted here that a "limiting move" is the opposite of what sometimes happens in long-term therapy. In the latter the patient presents a problem, and the therapist implies that beneath it lie other difficulties which the patient is just beginning to sense, and that these will act in subtle ways upon him. The patient now no longer worries about the problem that brought him, a "mere symptom," and shifts his focus to "more significant issues."

In my experience I have found it helpful to take the opportunity to suggest to the patient that not only is he fine in other areas of functioning, but that if he can conquer the problem now bothering him he may find lots of other areas in which he might notice an improvement of functioning. This has been called "the ripple effect" (see chapter 7). Sometimes a patient comes for a specific problem—perhaps he wishes to stop smoking—and then reports later, after he has been discharged from treatment, that his lifelong habit of nail biting has been cured, too. He may have become more assertive at work and asked for a raise, or he may have found that a neurotic symptom about which he did not tell you (e.g., fear of elevators) has disappeared.

There is nothing mysterious about the ripple effect. Once a patient is mobilized and regains confidence in his ability to solve problems, he sometimes finds that he can tackle other difficulties. The ripple effect has been reported in cases in which there was no mention of it beforehand. I find that, in discussing with the patient the fact that I usually like to obtain a follow-up telephone conversation sometime after treatment has ended, I also have the opportunity to insert unobtrusively a suggestion about the ripple effect if I care to. I do so in the hope that by alerting the patient to the effect I might enhance it.

The ripple effect is actually the opposite of "symptom substitution," about which many sophisticated patients have heard. That is, instead of finding problems emerging in formerly intact areas of functioning, as reported in instances of symptom substitution, adaptive coping learned in one area during psychotherapy becomes apparent in other areas as well. Symptom substitution, which will be considered at greater length in chapter 7, *can* be observed in certain contexts. However, it is by no means the ubiquitous phenomenon that early psychoanalytic theory postulated in clinical settings where "only" the presenting problem, rather than the "total personality," was treated.

BRIEFING THE PATIENT

The patient is not prepared for long-term therapy. In fact, many therapists find that patients are not sure what to expect, except what they can guess from the model of experiences with general medical doctors. It is generally necessary to inform the patient or family that in strategic therapy the patient will receive a number of directives, and that the success of therapy hinges on their implementation. "Homework" is introduced at the outset. Other aspects of therapy, such as its expected (short) duration, the interval between sessions, and such practical issues as fees, should also be discussed at the outset.

There are additional concerns that must be broached if a patient has had previous therapy. If the patient was dissatisfied, it is best to let him talk as long as he wishes about this experience without becoming defensive yourself. I once saw a woman whose previous therapist had suggested that they take showers together in order to increase her sense of intimacy. Originally such reports were dismissed as fantastic stories told by patients for their own reasons, but, as Masters and Johnson (1970, pp. 388–391) have suggested, they are numerous enough to grant them some credence. On the other hand, if the patient was extremely satisfied, it is a good idea to get some idea of what was so successful in the previous therapy.

As already mentioned, even if a patient has not formerly seen a therapist, in most instances he has attempted, unsuccessfully, to solve the problem on his own or with the help of family or friends. It is helpful at the outset for the therapist to find out what the patient's unsuccessful efforts had entailed.

A patient spoke to me about the fact that she had begun to gain weight after having done very well in a weight loss program. She was eating a great deal late at night, not "junk food" but solid meals. The problem seemed to be that she could not keep herself out of the kitchen at eleven or twelve at night. What she neglected to tell me before she asked for my advice is that after she had gained about four pounds on her usual sensible diet, she had adopted a strategy of starving herself all day long. What this strategy did was to make her so hungry at night that her hunger was strong enough to overcome her will power. If I had not stumbled on this fact, it would have been impossible to advise her. In this case she was able to lose weight by "paradoxically" eating breakfast, lunch, and dinner. Then she was not hungry and could keep herself out of the kitchen in the late night hours.

Almost all patients have tried or are trying something to help themselves, but sometimes they are shy about telling a therapist. For example, a patient with anxiety attacks might have tried prayer. Another patient might have deprived himself of his favorite candy until he could achieve his goal. Some patients may be drinking or taking drugs.

Since this subject was discussed in the previous chapter from the point of view of the patient, we need say little about it here other than to emphasize the need to understand what the patient has been doing up to the point of seeking therapy. Sometimes the therapist might just want to indicate that he thinks the patient's efforts are a good idea and ought to be continued.

THE USE OF BIOGRAPHICAL MATERIAL

In contrast to psychodynamic therapy, the collection of biographical material functions as a "data base" in strategic therapy, analogous to the screening tests and history compiled in the workup of a medical patient. It serves to identify the social class and background of the patient, and this helps to plan how one might phrase certain explanations or prescriptions. It helps to clarify the presenting complaint and to identify any other problems that might be contributory. The process of collecting this information need not occupy a major portion of initial interviews. Several questionnaires are available that patients can take home and fill out; alternatively, the patient can be asked to write a brief outline of important life events or a more extensive autobiography. While patients are apt to be offended if asked to do this before the initial interview, as it might seem too mechanical or impersonal, they are usually quite willing to respond subsequently.

FAILURE OF RECALL

One reason why psychotherapy is a more complex undertaking than may be expected initially is that a relatively small portion of patients do not recall or report information that the therapist would find useful, and therefore part of the therapeutic task can entail its discovery or recovery. There are several reasons why this state of affairs prevails. Not all patients are good observers or reporters. Sometimes this situation can be corrected by the therapist himself, who may be able to obtain samples of relevant behavior in his office when conjoint sessions are employed (e.g., husband and wife interact in the therapist's office) or if home visits are made. At other times a patient can be encouraged or taught to present more undigested or imaginative data or to find new memories that are relevant. At times necessary data are purposefully withheld. On a smaller number of occasions such secrets are pathogenic in and of themselves.

The great majority of patients can report what is bothering them. The small but distinct remainder who cannot seem to have served as the point of departure for psychoanalysis. Although psychoanalytic theory proposes repression as an explanatory concept for this small remainder of patients, Benedickt (cited in Ellenberger 1966) suggested that at least a portion of them were burdened by a "pathogenic secret." In this eventuality the patient is perfectly aware of what is troubling him, but does not tell others because he feels that it is unacceptable. Such patients can obtain relief through confession. Lazare, Eisenthal, and Wasserman (1975) have found what appears to be a fair proportion of patients entering a psychiatric clinic who are seeking such confessional release.

Several of Freud's early cases (Breuer and Freud 1895) did not report to him important aspects of the genesis of their symptoms because of a second reason: The incident that triggered a subsequent downhill course appeared trivial at the time. It was not that they had forgotten or repressed any important information, but rather that the interview technique, which depended upon a rather formal and rational discussion, was not the modality best designed to recover the required material. In a paper on hysteria I have reported that by the time a person suffering from a hysterical conversion reaction has been referred through a chain of repetitive, hostile, and psychologically inept medical evaluations designed to rule out organic pathology, he very often sounds like a medical chart (Rabkin 1964). He is likely to begin his presentation with "I am a nineteen-year-old single, white male. . . ." Freud's (Breuer and Freud 1895) solution to this interview problem was to shift from a verbal to a visual modality. With a hypnotic cermony such a patient was told that when he put his hand on his forehead or counted to five, an image, word (image of a word), or thought connected to the problem would pop into his head. As an alternative to Freud's image technique I have found that, when a hysteric presents, if I immediately and carefully explain that I am interested in "psychology" and not his medical case, and couple this with encouragement about his ability to remember relevant psychological details, I can usually get the patient to report such details.

After eliminating pathogenic secrets or patients who do not report psychologically relevant details for one reason or another, there still remains a group of patients who "have put out of their mind" certain traumatic thoughts or events. The patient with amnesia or in a fugue state is an example. One of the problems with asking a patient to remember the circumstances of the origin of a particular symptom is that it can be associated with unpleasant memories that are likely to cause pain, discomfort, or threats to his self-esteem or values. While some people tend to brood over traumatic events, other people tend to "forget" them. It has been pointed out that such self-serving "forgetting" is not so much an illustration of failure of memory as the acquisition of the "skill of not remembering," or putting material out of one's mind. In other words, there is a distinction between finding it difficult to retrieve some known item of information at the end of a long, tiring day (forgetting), and not putting together blatantly obvious hints that would culminate in a painful discovery. There has always been a question whether the recovery of such "forgotten" material resembles remembering or whether the term "reconstruction" is more accurate. Freud (1918, p. 122) referred to this as the most delicate question in all of psychoanalysis. Dollard and Miller (1950) assume that stopping a train of thought is similar in form to stopping a train of behavior as a result of fear. They illustrate their point with the example of someone with a mild fear of heights who is given the task of jumping across a four-foot gap from the roof of a skyscraper to a ledge two feet wide. He might well run up to the edge and suddenly find himself physically unable to jump. They emphasize that a train of thought is similar to running. It is not possible to expect someone to recount a fearful experience such as a war trauma unless something is done to reduce the fear, such as an injection of sodium amobarbital. It is assumed that some subjects cannot report anxiety-provoking stimuli for the same reason.

In what Ellenberger (1970) calls the First Dynamic Psychiatry, associated with Charcot, Janet, Breuer, Moebius, and the early work of Freud, much was made of the patient who forgot some crucial event, usually traumatic, which, when it was ultimately recovered, cured the patient of his symptoms. This model of recovery has its roots in eighteenth-century work with animal magnetism. With hypnosis the patient could be brought back to the original circumstances of the trauma and corrections made in his reaction so that symptoms did not recur. In most cases the model required that the patient experience again the intense emotions of the trauma—the fear experienced when one's horses ran wild with one's carriage, for example.

Motivated or learned forgetting in patients was also the point of departure for the Second Dynamic Psychiatry, of which Freud's later work is the most prominent example. Freud's vocabulary developed for his early work with the First Dynamic Psychiatry has been accepted as the terminology we now use in the Second Dynamic Psychiatry. For example, we refer to memories as "repressed," while Janet was more likely to say that they "migrated." We refer to the intense emotional display that is encouraged when such memories are recovered as "catharsis," while Janet used the more colorful term "moral fumigation." Over and above the use of Freud's terms, psychoanalytic thinking has extended the scope of that which is recovered from a traumatic or unpleasant event to that which is traumatic only insofar as it relates to certain species-wide themes like the castration fears associated with the Oedipus complex.

In order to clarify these different aspects of the use of biographical material, I shall discuss the discovery of new memories, secrets, the recovery of old memories, and Freud's concept of memory, followed by an examination of intense emotional display.

THE STIMULATION OF MEMORY IMAGES: NEW MEMORIES

It is possible that patients who are excellent reporters have selected well from the copious data of their lives and have put together a correct, or at least useful, abstraction of their problem and its background. However, few patients are excellent reporters. Instead, many present clichés or "memories" that they have been thinking about for decades, with no modification to take into account the recent problem that brought them into therapy. A third type of patient presents less digested and rehearsed material that allows for a more creative approach to its interpretation.

It is sometimes possible to ask certain imaginative patients to go "back" to a particular time or experience and relive it in the imagination. If this is done with ceremony, and the experience dates from the more distant past, the technique is called "hypnotic age regression." In this manner a patient can sometimes give information that would be unavailable if requested in a direct report. This is not material covered by amnesia, or purposefully excluded from recall, but it is not readily available because the patient hasn't thought about it recently.

Age regression has been regarded in two ways: as merely a feat of the imagination, and as an actual temporary ablation of subsequent stages of psychic development. Hypnotists generally seem to believe that when a subject is regressed to childhood, he has the characteristics of a child. This is presumably demonstrable if hypnotized regressed subjects do better than the adult mean on a task which is usually done better by children, such as an imbedded figure test. However, such performances seldom convince nonbelievers. This issue need not concern us here since we are merely interested in age regression as a means of recovering biographical material. (I regard age regression as imaginative role playing with good recall.)

Technically, age regression is simply an extension of the technique of stimulating a patient's memory by asking him to imagine where he was standing on a particular occasion, what the scene looked like, and so on, before asking for a specific desired fact. In age regression the patient is told he will go back in time to a stated age. It is helpful to specify a particular day, such as a birthday, Christmas, or Easter. Some clinicians specify the time of day. The patient is told that he will feel exactly as he did on that occasion, that he will see the same things he did then, and have the same experiences. It is best to wait a few minutes for the suggestion to sink in. However, no special skills are required for the effective use of this method if the subject is susceptible to it. It has been estimated (Spiegel 1972) that 10 to 15 percent of patients seeking psychotherapy are capable of age regression; in the individual case this can be determined by the ease of trance induction. (See Appendix B for Wolberg's [1945] age-regression method.)

In my practice I saw a woman of thirty who, when regressed with a hypnotic ceremony to age six, began to cry about the fact that her mother liked her sister better than herself. Her age regression was questionable—for example, she did not talk like a six-year-old. However, she was surprised by her own emotional reaction, having apparently lost touch with her feelings from that time until she put herself back into the situation. There was no evidence of an amnestic or other strategy designed to obliterate those traumatic times.

A similar method can also be used in the recovery of more recent information. In 1975, when nationally known former Teamster leader James Hoffa mysteriously disappeared, a witness was hypnotized in order to help him remember details of a conversation he had with Hoffa shortly before the latter's disappearance. Placing a person in the original situation can be a strategy to facilitate recall. Here again, there is no evidence of amnesia or deliberate forgetting.

An alternate strategy involves the use of imagery without a hypnotic ceremony. Here the patient is asked merely to imagine something, and is told that an image will pop into his mind that has some relevance to the desired data.

THERAPY OF THE SECRET BY THE SECRET

Another source of information is material that is deliberately kept secret by the patient. Although confession as a means of relieving suffering has an ancient and honorable theological history, it wasn't until the end of the nineteenth century that this phenomenon was noted in the medical literature by Benedikt (cited in Ellenberger 1966). He believed that certain people, such as those who had no chance to develop their abilities, or who lacked recognition from their peers, or who were very different from the people around them, developed a "second life" which they kept secret and which was sometimes burdensome. Sharing it with another person—a confessor—who was sworn to secrecy was regarded as an effective method of relief. Penitence (assumption of tasks to work off guilt) and absolution (bestowal of divine forgiveness) were not emphasized by Benedikt, but are also part of the confession ceremony.

Benedikt was mentioned by Freud in his work on hysteria because at times their thoughts were similar. However, Benedikt thought that both Freud and Janet relied too heavily on the notion of amnesia. He himself thought that much of the material recovered by hypnosis had not been forgotten but was merely held secret by the patient. For him the ceremony of hypnosis served largely as an excuse for the patient to unburden himself.

Jung (1963), in his autobiography, recalled that when he was a resident he examined a young woman who had been diagnosed as schizophrenic. Her word association tests suggested to him, however, that there was a gloomy story which she finally revealed to him. She had loved a man who did not seem to care for her, and as a result she married someone else. Five years later she heard that the man had in fact loved her too. She became despondent and, while bathing her little girl, absent-mindedly allowed the child to suck a dirty sponge. Her daughter developed typhoid fever and died. The mother was eventually hospitalized, having told nobody of these sad events. Jung explained to her that her illness was caused by the "pathogenic secret." Two weeks later she was discharged as cured. At the time Jung felt obliged to keep her secret, as a religious confessor is obliged, and subsequently spoke of this as the "therapy of the secret by the secret."

AMNESIA

Some people who are motivated and imaginative can utilize a strategy, either discovered or suggested, by which they can forget something which ordinarily cannot be forgotten, such as the number four (see Spanos' work, discussed in chapter 4). This material, removed from awareness by an induced amnesia, can be recovered through hypnosis. Usually, however, amnesias occur spontaneously. The forgotten material may be trivial or broad in scope. On rare occasions one sees a patient who has forgotten his identity altogether. Agatha Christie, the mystery writer, forgot who she was and was found several days later in a hotel under an assumed name. The resulting publicity was so distressing to her that she refused to give press interviews for years thereafter. The possibility of humiliating amnestic or fugue state patients must be kept in mind. Although their identity may be recovered through hypnosis, the procedure may not be appreciated by them. Often such patients will recover their memories spontaneously in a few days, which is considerably less embarrassing.

It is not the patient who has totally forgotten his identity who is most important for psychotherapists, in view of the rarity of such a phenomenon, but rather the patient who has forgotten some biographical fact that is essential to the understanding of the problem for which he seeks help. For example, one of my patients, a twenty-eight-year-old woman, had been unhappy for several weeks, although she did not know why. Logically she should have been feeling wonderful. She had a good job, her social life was fine, and she was terminating therapy because she was coping so well with events. She was asked to close her eyes while I counted to five, following which she would have an image pop into her head that would be related to her mood. At the count of five, she began to laugh. "Creamed spinach" was the image that popped into her mind. It seemed ridiculous, but she was aware that her mother had made creamed spinach especially for her when she was a child. The patient then realized that she was feeling somewhat unprotected and desirous of being mothered. Subsequently, her distress lifted as she realized that she could go back to her mother and ask for creamed spinach or allow herself to be babied in other ways. (Her mother hemmed a skirt for her.) In this case we can assume that the patient was trying to ignore her feelings and put them out of her mind. It is also important to note that relief occurred, not as a result of the discovery of her desire to be mothered, but after her development of an adaptive strategy of limited and controlled "regression."

Janet (1925) in 1893 treated Achille, a patient who was possessed. He came from a superstitious environment in a remote French province and was eventually brought to the Salpetrierre in a state of furious agitation, cursing, speaking in the voice of the devil, and so on. According to his records, he had succumbed just after a short business trip. Janet hypnotized the patient with some difficulty and finally got the story that he had had an affair on the business trip. He had tried to forget the incident but became increasingly guilty, feared damnation, and then suddenly found himself possessed. Janet worked through what he called "fixed ideas," first under hypnosis and then when Achille was not hypnotized. Thereafter the patient reportedly remained cured.

In both these cases one can assume too quickly that something has been deliberately put out of awareness. The first patient cannot find why she is upset. When she is offered a technique that taps visual imagery rather than logical analysis, she can immediately describe her problem. If she had been putting her desire to be babied out of awareness with an amnestic strategy, it was not a very persistent one. Her problem may have been that she was trying too hard to use her logic, which told her she should now feel grown up and happy. Were she more familiar with the concept of adaptive regression, she might have been more hospitable to her desire to be taken care of by her mother.

There are two different problems of recall. The first consists of efforts to recover material which are ineffective because the patient is attempting a logical analysis that proceeds from an incorrect frame of reference. In this case, data can be gathered by shifting to a technique that suspends logical or critical thinking in favor of a loose, brain-storming session. This type of thinking has been called "lateral" rather than "vertical," "right-brained" as opposed to "left-brained," "associating from below" rather than "above," and "gut feelings" rather than "thoughts." Various techniques that emphasize imagery fit in this category. The second type of problem occurs when historical material is being kept out of awareness by an amnestic strategy on the patient's part or by the discomfort associated with its revival. In both cases we might loosely refer to the patient "remembering" something, but in brain-storming what is remembered is "new," while in the discomfort example it is "old."

Although most published reports leave us with doubts about whether amnestic strategies were employed, in clinical practice one can observe such a strategy in use. In a particular case the patient is like the amnesia victim who wants to recover his identity but prevents himself at the same time. Hypnosis might be able to reverse the amnestic strategy since many of the same processes are used. However, just as one should not make the amnesia victim reveal his identity, so one might respect the purpose of the patient's strategy in other forms of failure of recall. One possible approach is to hypnotize such a patient and either by direct command or through some imagery technique obtain the needed information. Then such a patient can be told that he can remember as much or as little as he wants to about what was said during the trance.

One interesting imagery technique is to spin a tale in which the patient is on a train trip alone through a remote European nation, picturesque but out-of-the-way. The patient is in a train compartment alone with an old, kindly priest. In the course of their conversation the patient becomes overwhelmed with the desire to tell this kindly, wise old priest the deepest secret that he has.

Perhaps the most common situation in which an amnestic strategy is employed occurs when one member of a marriage should be able to figure out that the other is having an extramarital affair but somehow doesn't. Sometimes the information is all but told to one spouse, but he or she seems able to overlook it. I saw as patients a couple in which the wife was having an affair. The husband claimed to know nothing about it, but did find an excuse to seek marital counseling. Several years later, after the marriage had terminated, the husband returned to see me about a personal problem. I asked whether he had known of the affair. He said he had not, but that on some level he must have been aware of what was going on. For example, whenever he passed a motel that was near his house, he would check to see if his wife's car was parked there. This sort of information suggests that he did know of the affair but was putting it out of his mind. This is often the case with affairs: the spouse usually knows enough to suspect something, but often does not carry the line of thought to its logical conclusion. Husbands may claim, for example, to be spending nights on the couch at work when there is no couch in their offices. But many partners prefer to overlook or ignore such data, rather than confront it, so the material is excluded from awareness.

ARCHAEOLOGY

Using Janet's conceptualizations as a basis, Freud elaborated the notion of material covered by an amnesia. The task of the therapist evolved in his method from the finding of complete memories or facts to the analysis of clues, digging into the past, and reconstruction from memory fragments that Freud considered analogous to an archaeologist's task. Using the psychoanalytic method, the reconstructed facts became predominantly sexual in context, and ultimately species-wide in their structure.

Freud wrote extensively about his "archaeological" reconstructions of memories in his clinical cases. In one famous case a patient referred to as S. P. entered treatment with Freud in 1910 at the age of twenty-three and remained for four years (Freud 1918). During this time S. P. is reported to have "remembered" the following hitherto forgotten facts of his childhood and infancy in what must be one of the most outstanding feats of memory ever recorded. Although, as the celebrated case of the Wolf Man, his case history is said to represent a watershed in the development of psychoanalysis, it is instructive here in terms of our discussion of different types of biographical material recovered from patients.

As reconstructed from a dream of white wolves sitting in a walnut tree together with other analytic material, the following events were delineated *as a memory*: On a hot summer afternoon when he was one and a half years of age the patient was asleep on a cot in his parents' bedroom. At five o'clock he awoke with a malarial attack to witness his mother and father having sexual intercourse three times in white underclothes (hence white wolves). The first time sex was in the conventional position. After this the position was altered to one in which coitis was performed from behind with the father upright and the mother bent down. The patient finally deliberately interrupted his parents by passing a stool which gave him an excuse for screaming.

The case, including several other significant early memories, was published by Freud soon after the analysis was completed. Freud, of course, described the drama of uncovering the events, some of which I have abstracted above, in beautifully written and convincing prose. I have always been amused at the disarming insouciance with which Freud ends his first partial revelation of the "primal scene trauma": "There is at bottom nothing extraordinary . . . in the fact that a young couple who had been married a few years should have ended a siesta on a hot summer's afternoon with a love-scene . . ." True, there is nothing remarkable in that—but that the little boy whose presence they had disregarded should remember it at age twenty-five? That is nothing but extraordinary.

What the case of S. P. illustrates, perhaps in its most enduring aspects, is what we do and do not mean by "memory." When we say that "mother had sex with father" and further certify our statement with "I *remember* mother had sex with father," we mean one of three things:

1. That we were witness to the event (as the Wolf Man declared).
2. That we believed the event to be plausible when it occurred from a variety of sources of data *from that time* and are now referring to that belief.
3. That we recently recovered bits and pieces of data apparently dating from that time which now allow us plausibly to assume that an event occurred. (This last method of remembering was invented by Freud. He compared it to archaeological reconstructions of past civilizations.)

Freud admitted that "the most delicate question in the whole domain of psychoanalysis" revolved around which of these three possibilities applies to material like that presented to us by the case of S. P.—whether it is eyewitnessing, remembering in the second sense, or in the entirely new sense he devised.

INTENSE EMOTIONAL FEELING: MORAL FUMIGATION

The recovery of new memories, secrets, or formerly amnestic or reconstructed biographical facts is usually not considered sufficient as a therapeutic goal. It must be followed by an intense emotional reaction or display. In most psychotherapy, as Marshall (1972) has reviewed, the essential moments of therapy are conceived of as relating to the release of supposedly dammed-up painful emotions, which in turn are supposed to stem from the forgotten biographical material.

The terms "abreaction" and "catharsis" were used by Freud to describe those moments of release that were conceptualized as curing the patient of dammed-up emotions. Janet, who probably deserves credit for the concept, used the more colorful term "moral fumigation," but this term lacks the scientific quality that Freud was able to add to his studies. (Janet, a teacher of philosophy, still imbued his terms with the connotions which placed psychology within philosophy as a subcategory of morals.) Here is Freud's first use of the terms:

> The injured person's reaction to the trauma only exercises a completely "cathartic" effect if it is an adequate reaction—as for instance, revenge. But language serves as a substitute for action; by its help, an affect can be "abreacted" almost as effectively. In other cases speaking is itself the adequate reflex, when, for instance, it is a lamentation or giving utterance to a tormenting secret, e.g., a confession. If there is no such reaction, whether in deeds or words, or in the mildest cases in tears, any recollection of the event retains its affective tone to begin with (Breuer and Freud 1895, p. 8).

Freud goes on to say that in a "normal" person, even without abreaction or catharsis the memory of a trauma becomes diluted by what follows. If the memory was of danger, it is diluted in terms of the rescue and subsequent safety. Among normal people traumatic memories are also said to fade. But in his hysterical patients Freud noticed that the traumatic memories were astonishingly vivid and fresh. He attributed this to two causes: (1) the nature of the trauma, which excluded an immediate reaction; and (2) the patient's special state of consciousness (semihypnotic twilight) when the trauma occurred (see chapter 5).

These patients were thought to suffer from "retention" hysterias, that is, retention of the emotions associated with the past trauma. War traumas during both World Wars I and II were extensively studied in terms of the retention and abreaction concepts. Proponents of the release-of-dammed-up-emotions theory felt that release of the strong emotional forces was essential to relief. However, others pointed out that operationally what was required was a strong emotional *display*, and results were proportional to this display. The retention notion, the concept that the cause was the unreleased emotion, was conjecture but could not be proved. As Marshall has said, "Some practitioners felt it was not even important that the events recalled be accurate as long as the emotion was released" (1972, p. 787). The experimental work on this point does not unequivocally support the retention (also known as reservoir) theory. In addition, logically, the reservoir theory would not require the presence of another person, but merely the emotional outlet. Crying to oneself would fit the requirements of the theory, yet every commentator has believed that catharsis and abreaction must occur in the presence of an "understanding" person. It is entirely possible that such a person, in the context of being understanding, subtly prescribes certain behaviors, a ceremony that relieves the patient's burden.

Although few psychoanalysts now feel that the "one-shot" release of emotions is of any lasting therapeutic value, Marshall believes that most dynamic therapists implicitly, if not explicitly, adhere to the primacy of emotional discharge as an explanation for the relief of suffering, while experimentalists are increasingly skeptical of this view.

As I shall disuss in the next chapter, an intense emotional experience is frequently expected by patients and often induced by certain interview techniques. As such, it functions to impress the patient with the significance of what is happening. It boosts his morale and faith in the therapeutic process, and in this way has salutary effects on treatment.

Freud's use of the terms "abreaction" and "catharsis" includes many processes. First he suggests that the only adequate reaction to trauma is something like revenge. In the chapter on the transfer of suffering (chapter 7) this strategy will be discussed at length and evaluated. Freud also includes mourning (lamentation) and confession. In his discussion quoted above, "abreaction" is left as another distinct substitute for action which is not clearly defined. It has come to mean the display of intense emotional feelings to a sympathetic therapist.

The concept has become so popular that it has taken on the quality of a life style. Openness, "letting it all hang out," and expressing oneself freely have been taken by a distinct segment of society as a preferred way of relating to others. Unfortunately tact, preciseness of expression, privacy, and subtle coloration of one's statements have had to suffer in what one commentator referred to as "psychobabble" (Rosen 1975).

In at least one situation, that of bereavement, it has been demonstrated that emotional expression facilitates eventual recovery from the trauma. In most cases the presence of a supportive network of friends is sufficient to assure that adequate mourning will take place. When this is not possible, either because of the lack of a sufficient network or because the loss itself is not widely accepted as sufficient to warrant such attention, other strategies must be employed by the patient. For example, a patient terminated her relationship with a boyfriend and was very upset. She expected that she would have some difficulty sleeping and concentrating on work, which had been her experience in the past. However, the patient decided "not to run away from the experience" and deliberately went about intensifying her unhappy feeling. She purchased several volumes of love poems which caused her to cry copiously. She even wrote her own poetry. The result was that she slept well and, when she was at work, found herself absorbed and productive. In such a case it is necessary at times to terminate mourning ceremoniously at some point. If a bereaved person wore black, a formal return to normal clothing would serve to terminate the mourning stage. Analogous terminations are helpful in smaller losses as well.

CHAPTER 3

A Horse in the House: The Problem of Compliance

A HARRIED MAN once sought the advice of his rabbi. He complained that his children were rowdy, his wife bickered all the time with them, his mother-in-law insisted on her own room, and that at the end of a hard day spent taking care of the farm, his little house was really a very unpleasant, crowded place to which to come home.

The rabbi's solution was ingenious. Each week he asked the man to bring *into the house* a new animal from his barnyard: the horse, the cow, the goat, and so on. Following the introduction of each new member into the household, the rabbi dutifully asked how the farmer was feeling and received the obvious answer. After all the animals on the farm were living in his house, the rabbi suggested that the farmer should now remove one animal at a time. When he had finally removed each and every animal, the rabbi once again asked how he felt. The farmer responded that it was a joy to live with his children, his wife, and his mother-in-law—his loving, active family.

Although the solution was a clever one, the real question is how did the rabbi get the farmer to bring the animals in the house in the first place? The critical problem is more often not to find the right solution, but to get the patient to accept and follow it. People frequently do not follow advice, whether it is given by a clergyman or a doctor. Data have been compiled to show that, on the average, patients take only about half the dosages prescribed for them, and in some cases fail to take as much as 90 percent of their prescribed medication (Boyd et al. 1974).

The problem of noncompliance is not restricted to the taking of medication, which constitutes a comparatively straightforward and easily understood task. Any request made of a demoralized patient is apt to be carried out halfheartedly or not at all, even if he understands and accepts its validity. In psychotherapy I would estimate that about one-third of one's patients will not readily comply with instructions. Since brief therapy depends heavily on the patients' completion of assigned tasks, the problem of compliance represents an important consideration in this therapeutic approach.

Physicians in medical settings often do not seem too concerned about compliance. Although a patient may not follow his instructions, the average physician doesn't change his approach or try very hard to do much about it. It is true that most patients probably do what they are told, and one's attention and efforts can be addressed to this majority. Such a position is actually recommended in a triage situation where not everyone can be treated, and selection on some basis is essential. If it is necessary or desirable to use the least amount of personnel in the most effective fashion, compliant patients might deserve priority.

In extreme forms, resistance to treatment may become a major preoccupation of the patient, and he may successfully discourage any efforts to negotiate with him. For example, a colleague reported that a man came to see him who had already interviewed twelve other therapists for the honor of treating him. In this initial interview it became rapidly apparent that this was a most difficult and resistant individual. My colleague did not trouble to figure out how to capture this man for treatment, and was relieved when the patient went on to interview the four-teenth therapist.

Not all noncompliant patients are difficult people. In some cases the physician's instructions are so extreme that they virtually guarantee failure in their execution, no matter how obedient the patient tries to be. Common examples are found in stringent diets given to patients, such as those for the diabetic in the days before insulin, or the strict ban on salt often imposed on hypertensive patients. In other instances, particularly in some varieties of brief therapy, the patient is asked to do something which seems incompatible with common sense. While such instructions may be dramatically effective if the patient complies without critical reflection, they may fail in other cases. One successful example of uncommonsense advice is cited by Erickson (in Haley 1967, p. 42), whose young son had been hurt and needed emergency suturing. All the way to the surgeon's office the father explained to his son that his injury was really not large enough to warrant as many stitches as his sister had received at the time of her hand injury. The child was urgently counseled and exhorted that it would be entirely his responsibility to see to it that the surgeon put in as many stitches as possible; he was thoroughly coached on how to demand his full rights. When they arrived the surgeon, in puzzled silence, sutured the laceration without anesthesia as the child demanded that the sutures be placed closer together.

In general, there are two levels of approach to the induction of compliance in the context of brief psychotherapy; they may be referred to as the direct and the indirect methods. That used by Erickson in the above example was indirect. He did not try to inform his son about the nature of the pain relief strategy, but instead manipulated the situation in such a way that the boy behaved according to his plan. In contrast, a direct approach is one that informs a patient what he should do to deal with his problem or symptom, and in some cases also offers the underlying rationale. Thus in pain relief, one can openly tell a patient that his experience of pain will be reduced if he participates actively in the treatment, as demonstrated in the training that has been devised for natural childbirth. The rest of this chapter illustrates varieties of direct and indirect techniques for the induction or enhancement of compliance in the therapeutic situation.

The therapist must choose between the direct and the indirect approaches for influencing patients. Both methods involve exerting as much influence on the patient as can be achieved and still remain effective. There are certain therapists, such as Erickson (in Haley 1973a) and the Palo Alto group including Fisch, Weakland, and Watzlawick (Weakland et al. 1974), who almost always opt for an indirect approach. Others, such as Gillis (1974), prefer direct methods of influencing patients. It is an illusion to assume that you do not influence a patient. The question is only how it is done, and whether it is done well or badly.

At the present time no clear-cut guidelines can be offered about when to use a direct or an indirect approach. The choice depends both on the therapist's personal style and preferences, and on the type of patient and problem he is called upon to treat. Some patients have histories of noncompliance, and certain conditions such as anorexia or obesity suggest problems in this area. For most patients, the ordinary process of psychotherapy is sufficient to evoke adequate levels of cooperation so that special techniques for enhancing compliance are not indicated. However, there are enough potentially noncompliant patients to warrant consideration of the methods described here in order to make their treatment feasible.

DIRECT METHODS

While the general professionalism of one's approach is perhaps the major factor supporting the patient's expectation that he will benefit from therapy, certain behavior on the part of the thera-

pist can specifically increase that expectation and thereby pro-
mote compliance. Some of these have been found in a hit-or-
miss fashion, often having rationales that do not explicitly take
into account the issues of motivation, locus of control, or the
deliberate boosting of spirits. Others are frankly employed for
that effect. Gillis has, perhaps, been the most candid about various techniques and ploys to this end. He wrote, "To achieve
influence from the start, the therapist should make every effort
to enhance the patient's expectation of benefit. He can develop
ploys beyond the wildest dreams of a used car salesman" (Gillis
1974, p. 91).

Examples of the techniques to which he refers will be discussed in turn. Ordeals, the prestige of the therapist, explaining
to others, the therapist's obvious belief in himself, the personal
interest shown in the patient, interpretations, and the experiencing of intense emotions during the session each serve to mobilize
the patient.

ORDEALS

If a patient works, travels, or suffers before getting to see the
therapist or during the course of therapy, he will have a greater
expectation of benefit than if things are made easy and accessi-
ble for him. The role of a pilgrimage in the search for a cure has
long been recognized, especially in a religious context, as in the
case of Lourdes. I understand that no permanent resident of the
city of Lourdes has ever been helped there. The point is vividly
expressed by Torrey (1973), who compares the experiences of
two hypothetical men. A depressed, middle-aged man from New
England arrives by taxi at the door of the Menninger Clinic in
Topeka, Kansas. It has been a difficult trip including two planes,
and considerable financial sacrifice is entailed. Another
depressed, middle-aged man from West Africa arrives by
crowded bus from up-country to an African healing shrine. It
has been a difficult trip for him, too, including a day of walking,
two buses, and much financial sacrifice. As he starts up the hill

toward the famous shrine, he feels better. He has hope. As the New Englander enters the clinic door he also begins to feel better; he too, has hope. Both men have been mobilized by their pilgrimage.

Other obstacles besides distance frequently block access to a therapist, fees and time being the most prominent. Psychoanalysis, to take an extreme example, usually entails several visits a week over a period of years and may cost over $15,000. Even when treatment is less prolonged and fees are largely covered by insurance, therapists and clinics may have long waiting lists or inconvenient daytime appointment hours. People are often reluctant to take time off from work regularly because of their unwillingness to have it known that they are receiving psychiatric treatment.

While most mental health professionals regard waiting lists and awkward appointment hours as regrettable if unavoidable conditions, Gillis actually advocates their occasional use to enhance the patient's determination to receive treatment. He has even arranged for "noxious" psychological tests to be administered repeatedly to increase the patient's ordeal. While such artificial obstacles may be needed or useful for the average therapist, widely known therapists have no need to invent difficulties for prospective patients, since their full schedules and reduced accessibility serve this purpose. One consequence is that highly successful therapists see only patients who are extremely persistent and eager for their help. The busier one's practice, the more motivated are the patients by the time they finally succeed in getting an appointment. When he practiced in New York, Erich Fromm was virtually impossible to reach. Those patients who managed to get in touch with him were both highly committed to treatment with him and not particularly demoralized or incapacitated.

The problem clinically is to offer obstacles which the patient will surmount and thereby increase his commitment and his hope. Too great an obstacle will either discourage patients from even trying to get help, or will drive them away after they have experienced an initial rebuff. Indeed, some patients are so unmotivated or hesitant that it is sometimes necessary to remove the smallest hindrance in the path to treatment; outreach programs designed to serve selected unmotivated patients such as the discharged chronic schizophrenic go to such lengths as arranging for food to be given out in conjunction with clinic visits, or providing community care teams to seek out recalcitrant patients in their homes. However, in private practice and in most clinic settings only those patients who seek help and use their own initiative are seen. Among these, the "ordeal" strategy would seem to apply largely to those prospective patients who are of the middle or upper class, who are accustomed to getting what they want, and who are sufficiently intact to persist in their goal-seeking behavior. Patients of this kind may even create their own ordeals. The man who flies past thousands of competent doctors to seek out a particularly valued consultant or treatment center (e.g., the Mayo Clinic) is manipulating his own expectations without knowing it. For those with fewer resources, either personal, social, or material, the ordeal process may not be the strategy of choice in creating an effective therapeutic milieu.

PRESTIGE WORK AND EXPLAINING TO OTHERS

The more famous the therapist, the more he is regarded as a "big doctor," the more a patient expects to benefit. If he has a busy schedule, is a consultant to other doctors, if the secretary in a clinic mentions how lucky the patient is to be assigned to Dr. X "since most patients seem to prefer him," or if a patient overhears something special about a therapist, his prestige works for him. Torrey (1973) has pointed out that diplomas on the wall, slightly unusual dress, or an academic title each contribute to the prestige that the patient recognizes.

Prestige work consists of that which the therapist does to encourage the patient's belief that he is effective. I know of one

excellent specialist in rehabilitation medicine who has an unob-
trusive inscribed picture of President Kennedy, whom he treated,
hanging in his office. Every patient notices it and, needless to
say, is impressed. The doctor himself is quite modest when
asked about it. Whether they are aware of it or not, all therapists
do some prestige work, if it is only to the extent of hanging their
diplomas on the wall. The appropriate amount of prestige work
depends to some extent on the nature of one's clientele. Especially in a clinic setting or with a less prosperous and sophisticated population, too much prestige may make a prospective
patient feel that the therapist is not likely to care about him or
will not take time to do a good job. On the other hand, more
sophisticated and affluent patients are more likely to be sensitive
to pretensions on the part of the therapist, which will reduce
rather than enhance his stature in their eyes.

Related to the therapist's prestige is the fact that patients who
have gone to famous doctors like to talk about it. They like to
explain to others about their problems and about the effectiveness of their therapist and his methods. As Gillis (1974) has
pointed out, at the same time they explain to others they are tai-
loring the explanation to themselves. As with other subjects,
when one teaches it, one finally comes to learn it. Keeping this
in mind, Gillis has asked patients to explain the principles of
psychotherapy to other patients. In the course of converting
others they convert themselves.

SELF-CONFIDENCE OF THERAPIST

An issue closely related to the prestige of the therapist is his
own belief in himself. One can have great prestige and be cyni-
cal or, one might say, merely realistic about one's powers. However, if a therapist is enthusiastic about his ability, this is transmitted to the patient, with the result that the patient's hopes are
raised. Frank (1973) has reported evidence suggesting that the
first patient seen by a therapist in the course of a day is more apt

to improve than subsequent ones. The therapist is presumably more enthusiastic at the start of the day, and when the therapist has hope, the patient has hope.

Some therapists submit themselves to ordeals in the expectation that they will benefit just as patients do. For example, I once supervised a young, talented social worker who just didn't believe that he could do the work of a "real" therapist. He enrolled in an arduous and largely irrelevant training program, hoping to generate enough faith in himself to be able to go out into practice.

It is very difficult for a therapist to maintain the feeling that he can help the people who come to him when they keep coming back week after week without changing. Those therapists who see patients infrequently, like hypnotists, are much more apt to have the necessary élan, spirit, or faith in themselves necessary for rapid treatment procedures. The most successful cures tend to occur when therapist and patient share the expectation that the patient will get better. This has been found to apply to success from gastrectomies and eye operations as well as psychotherapy. An interesting sidelight to the question of faith in oneself is the frequently noticed occurrence that an inexperienced young therapist sometimes has a very high success rate with cases deemed hopeless by his superiors. In such cases it must be the beginner's eagerness, enthusiasm, and optimism, rather than skill or experience, that make the difference.

INTEREST SHOWN IN THE PATIENT

It is generally a good idea to consider how much interest shown in a patient will be therapeutic. Paranoids usually prefer to maintain some distance, perhaps because they expect that those who try to be friendly will eventually betray them (see chapter 8). Most patients, however, appear to have seemingly inconsistent expectations. They want to go to a doctor who is special, who has great prestige, who is busy and inaccessible, yet at the same time they want this doctor to show a personal interest in them. It is of no value to have an inept therapist really care about you, nor is it helpful to have an Einstein of a therapist who shows no interest.

Those who teach student therapists tend to emphasize either one aspect or the other. Some stress the importance of a dignified therapeutic stance and the significance of a professional demeanor. Others emphasize the effect of being "genuine, warm, and empathetic." The integration of these two qualities, which characterizes some of the finest therapists, is largely the product of experience and maturity in the therapeutic role. This combination is ultimately the most effective. Thus, if "Kennedy's back doctor" remembers your name and something personal about you, it has a powerful effect on your expectation that he will be able to help you and that your problems are nearing an end.

INTERPRETATIONS

Of paramount importance in the thinking of some therapists is an intervention called "an interpretation." Among many psychodynamically oriented psychotherapists, interpretations are regarded as the crucial therapeutic element because insight is regarded as synonymous with cure. There are other ways to look at interpretations. One source of the effectiveness of an interpretation is its ability to convince the patient that his doctor is brilliant and perceptive, and therefore likely to treat him successfully. When one hears the content of the interpretation that was so insightful, one is frequently impressed with the fact that the remark could apply to almost anyone. This sort of "no-miss" or "Aunt Fanny" interpretation (applicable to you, me, or my Aunt Fanny) is frequently quite effective. Of course we like to think that interpretations are more than that, and perhaps at times they are. At present I am only discussing interpretations from a contextual perspective. Here are some examples of no-miss interpretations:

1. Underneath that anger there's an awful lot of hurt.
2. You seem to want to be the best at everything you try.

3. A lot of your difficulties stem from the extraordinary demands you make on yourself. You can't always be successful.
4. You're living your life as an apology.
5. You don't realize how often you are intimidated by others.

Frank (1973) cites a study in which once a month a therapist offered the same interpretation to six patients, changing the interpretation each month. The patients reportedly prospered under this routine.

Snyder and Shenkel (1975) added a useful dimension to our understanding of the conditions that facilitate acceptance of no-miss interpretations. They distributed to subjects in their study the same set of astrological readings, psychological test results, and handwriting analyses. The more the subjects believed that these reports were prepared specifically for them, the more accurate they were perceived to be. Thus, when asked for the year, month, and day of their birth, they rated astrological reports of the no-miss variety as excellent, while subjects who did not provide this personalized information were more doubtful about the validity of the reports they were given. Apparently, then, almost any "Aunt Fanny" is acceptable if it seems to the patient to have been specifically developed for him, based on material he himself has provided. In a therapeutic context, an interpretation based on a dream would fit these requirements. While the therapist might make an interpretation that he has offered many times before, it will be accepted by a patient if it seems to stem from his own dream.

In the course of their study, Snyder and Shenkel used a personality summary which can be seen as a plausible description of most of us:

Some of your aspirations tend to be pretty unrealistic. At times you are extroverted, affable, sociable, while at other times you are introverted, wary, and reserved. You have found it unwise to be too frank in revealing yourself to others. You pride yourself on being an independent thinker and do not accept others' opinions without satisfactory proof. You prefer a certain amount of change and variety, and become dissatisfied when hemmed in by restrictions and limitations. At times you have serious doubt about whether you have made the right decision or done the right thing. Disciplined and controlled on the outside, you tend to be worrisome and insecure on the inside. Your sexual adjustment has presented some problems for you. While you have some personality weaknesses, you are generally able to compensate for them. You have a great deal of unused capacity which you have turned to your advantage. You have a strong need for other people to like you and for them to admire you (Snyder and Shenkel 1975, p. 53).

Notice that the paragraph contains mostly favorable remarks. Snyder and Shenkel found that favorable remarks are considered more accurate than critical ones.

Interpretations that clarify a situation for a patient or that compare one situation with another, as well as interpretations that are generated by the therapist's particular theory, can be helpful in the same fashion as no-miss interpretations. They can give the patient hope that, if the therapist is so perceptive or so brilliant as to be able to put things together, then he can be helpful in dealing with the problem. These two aspects of therapy are not necessarily related. For example, comparing a current problem with a past one does not necessarily lead to a solution to either one. Knowing how and "why" one got in jail does not get one out. However, it increases confidence in the therapist.

INTENSE EMOTION

An intense emotional display in the therapy session is helpful in the same fashion as an interpretation: it bolsters hope and fosters compliance. It is not necessary to accept the concept that cure follows the release of dammed-up emotions from the past. Even without this framework patients are impressed with an emotional session, frequently expect it, and occasionally attempt to create one by deliberately choosing to discuss areas of their life about which they know they feel bad (for example, the death of a parent), whether or not that subject is germane to the problem that brought them into therapy. When sessions are observed through one-way mirrors by other therapists, those in which there has been an emotional display are frequently judged to be more meaningful.

There are two general approaches that a therapist can employ to raise the emotional level of a session. The first is the manipulation of privacy. When a psychiatrist asks detailed questions about sexual behavior, secrets, or other extremely private material, some patients become tense and emotional, particularly if they do not have the utmost confidence in their therapist. However, seemingly innocuous material can also elicit strong feelings. I have known a patient to become nauseated after making a simple, obvious criticism of her mother ("she is fat"), because of a taboo against family criticism. At the other extreme, there are patients who "let it all hang out," who discuss everything "openly" as part of their general life style.

A second approach is to pick up hints of emotion and to license them, bring them out in the open. These usually occur in relation to the patient's chief complaint. Thus, by watching a patient's face one may see the eyes water when a particular subject is discussed. We are all exquisitely sensitive to these subtle changes in others, but usually for the purpose of avoiding emotion. Without intervention, the patient would probably hold back tears in the interest of following the usual rules of social discourse.

Once the therapist observes hints of emotion, there are two ways of bringing them out in the open: "attribution work" and "verbalizing." In attribution work the therapist attributes to the patient more than he sees. When one encourages a child to play the piano by saying he is doing marvelously and is playing the piano beautifully, when in fact he is just beginning to catch on, one *attributes* for effect more to the situation than is there. Similarly, when a patient's eyes well up, one can say, "You have a lot of crying to do." The patient, it must be noted, is not presently crying; his eyes are just a little watery. But the therapist does not say "Your eyes are watery," which is an accurate statement of fact; he attributes more to the situation than he sees, as if that, too, were fact.

The second possibility is that the patient can be asked to verbalize his feelings. Feelings follow behavior, even verbal behavior. The more one acts or verbalizes about a subject, the more strongly one feels about it. This sequence is not generally familiar to laymen. The man in the street assumes that first you are ("feel") angry and then you act angry, when, in fact, the reverse is frequently the case. Certain techniques of the human potential movement (encounters and so on) are particularly impressive to patients who are ignorant of the sequence. A common method is to have a patient imagine someone is in front of him (e.g., his mother) and shout angry remarks at her. What happens is that the patient begins to feel "real" rage, although he might have started by merely going through the motions. Method acting takes advantage of the same phenomenon.

Primal scream therapy can also be considered from the point of view of inducing intense emotional reactions. The technique shares many of the attributes of all therapies, such as the search for prestigious therapists and the experience of ordeals. However, its core method, consisting of asking the patient to lie in a vulnerable position and just repeat aloud a painful stimulus (e.g., "mother"), is an excellent way of inducing an intense emotional reaction.

Although intense emotional experiences during psychotherapy can be productive, too much intensity can detract from the effectiveness of treatment. Sullivan (1954) was particularly concerned that too much tension decreases the accuracy of information that the therapist is able to obtain. Tension can "hypnotize" a patient into "confessing" what he thinks the therapist wants to hear. Another risk is that emotional experiences can become ends in themselves, rather than a transitional step in a problem-solving sequence. An intense emotional experience that is overly long can also serve to precipitate a religious conversion experience. The patient becomes a true believer or sect member, an outcome that has been known to convert people into Freudians, Jungians, Primal Screamers, and so on. The price exacted under these circumstances for the relief of symptoms is obviously excessive.

In addition to the direct methods cited by Gillis and described above, there are several other direct ways of enhancing the patient's motivation to comply with therapeutic strategies. These include working with the patient's sense of urgency, the need for him to acknowledge the failure of prior efforts at problem solving, the timing of therapeutic intervention in a crisis situation, and the matter of licensing changes.

PERCEPTION OF URGENCY

In strategic therapy it is helpful if both patient and therapist perceive a moderate degree of urgency about solving a problem. It is well known that secondary gains associated with certain kinds of problems are sufficiently rewarding to make the problem itself tolerable to the patient. Sometimes the therapist can counteract this effect by delineating the nature and extent of the patient's *secondary losses*. A striking example is provided by Erickson (1962), who instructed a mother literally to sit on top of her unmanageable son all day long. The strategy itself is admittedly unusual. However, Erickson reminds the reader of something even more curious about the situation. How did he persuade a college-educated, middle-class mother to sit on her son as a solution to a psychological problem? Erickson encouraged her to imagine what would happen if her son continued to be totally undisciplined. She eventually concluded that he would wind up in an institution (a plausible outcome in this case). This created the urgency necessary for Erickson to obtain the mother's cooperation. In another case he allowed the patient, who felt he couldn't be helped, to reach the door on his way out before he suggested that there were one or two things that he might be willing to try.

At the other extreme, patients may present a problem about which the therapist does not share their sense of urgency. Some situations tend to be self-correcting or are resolved simply with the passage of time, especially certain developmental problems of childhood. In such cases the therapist can indicate both directly and by his relaxed manner that such a problem is not an urgent one.

While a sense of urgency about the problem is more or less indispensable to the therapeutic enterprise, it is an aspect that can be abused by therapists looking for business or by therapeutic movements seeking followers. I have seen parents who spent considerable time, money, and energy on "perceptual training" for their young son, performed by an optometrist who scared them into it with dire predictions that the boy would not do well in school at some future point. My ophthalmologist and educator friends tell me that such training is not indicated; certainly there is no justification for stating definitively that it will make the difference between school success and failure. The purpose of communicating a sense of urgency is to enhance the patient's motivation, not to capture business by manipulating his fears.

ADMITTING FAILURE

The patient must believe that he needs the therapist's help to solve his problem. He must therefore acknowledge that he can't solve it by himself, and that whatever efforts he has made in the past, alone or with helpers, have not been successful. Frequently this can be established simply by inquiring about what actions the patient has taken before seeking psychotherapy.

Minuchin (1974) has developed a technique for treating patients with anorexia nervosa that is partially based on this consideration. Characteristically, although the patient's parents seek help, they do not give up their own ineffective efforts to fatten up the patient. Minuchin's method is to invite the family to have lunch with him and allow them to repeat their usual, unsuccessful attempts to get the patient to eat. Minuchin underlines their failure as strongly as he can, and tries to get the parents to acknowledge that the patient has "won" again. There is more to Minuchin's treatment of the problem, but I feel that a crucial element is this emphasis on prior failure. In short, if a patient can acknowledge that he and perhaps others have failed up to this point in solving the problem, he will be more receptive to the therapist's prescriptions for a changed strategy. Certain self-help groups, such as Synanon, probably use this technique exclusively.

CRISIS INTERVENTION

Urgency and a sense of failure help motivate the patient. Sometimes these feelings occur spontaneously in a *crisis*. A crisis can be of two sorts. First, there is what one typically thinks of as a crisis—an accident, tragedy, or other sudden emergency. The second type of crisis has been referred to as a *growth crisis*. In this situation, stress is generated as a result of a transition from one status to another, such as getting married. I would extend this category to include such potentially stressful situations as migration, loss of a job, or any significant life event that requires substantial readjustment. An emergency requires immediate treatment, while a growth crisis is a time of danger and opportunity that may not require any intervention at all.

Watzlawick, Weakland, and Fisch (1974) have pointed out that most growth crises in our culture, although often difficult, are accompanied by social expectations that one should be having a wonderful time. The honeymoon, for example, and newly married life are apt to be stressful. Most divorces occur in the first five years, and most separations occur in the second year of marriage, yet we characteristically overlook the difficulties and romanticize this time of life. This might be excellent as a strategy, and perhaps is a cultural device somewhat like a strategy, but a therapist should be aware that there are times when it fails.

Normal growth crises can be stressful experiences; their failure to occur can also generate discomfort. Haley (1973a) has suggested that when one cannot find a behavioral goal in therapy, one should look for a transition that has *not* occurred. One of the most common patients to see a psychiatrist in private practice is probably the single woman of about thirty years of age who, although she may complain of anxiety or depression, is also suffering from being single, from a failure to change status. Her anxiety and depression may be approached by dealing with her single status, although she does not present with that complaint.

Crises facilitate compliance with authorities and the emergence of new behavior. One's usual resources and patterns of coping are no longer reliable methods for solving problems, and former rules seem less fixed. For example, when your car breaks down on the highway and a repairman comes, you have faith in him and are more likely to do what he suggests than if the same condition occurred when the car was in your garage and you were able to shop around for several estimates while remembering stories of overcharging and incompetence. Similarly, in a personal crisis the patient is more apt to be receptive and responsive and the therapist has greater influence. Therapeutic activity in this context can have a greater impact in a shorter period of time, and in recent years has been developed as a distinct branch of strategic psychotherapy because of its unique characteristics.

I believe that the essence of crisis intervention is responsiveness. In designing crisis intervention units, I have found that perhaps the most crucial element is development of a rapid response. In practice this means having enough telephone lines, answering services, and beepers (portable devices on which one can be called) to insure a rapid response to any telephone call.

In order to be responsive to the earliest signs of difficulty, one needs contacts in the community, "listening posts," as Auerswald (1971) called them. For example, police are frequently aware of difficult situations in the neighborhood which are not actually police matters, but which come to them because they, the fire department, and the hospital emergency room are the only facilities that most communities can contact which are always open and responsive. In the South Bronx of New York City there have been times when the fire department has been called to intervene in gang wars because they were the only ones likely to respond. In order to serve a meaningful role in the community and for individuals, a crisis intervention unit must acquire a similar reputation.

LICENSES

Patients may fail to cooperate in psychotherapy because of the influence of other significant people. Haley (1963) has referred to this as his First Law, which states that whenever one person makes a change, others will act so as to minimize that change. It is almost an automatic reaction within groups or systems. Jackson (1968) was the first to point out that these "homeostatic forces" can work against the therapy. Families, like other systems, tend to stabilize in certain patterns. Any therapeutic effort that might disrupt prevailing patterns is perceived as a threat. Sometimes an individual with a symptom can become part of the pattern of a family rather than a problem to it. An effort to aid the patient will affect the relationships among others in the family, who are then apt to resist change in the patient.

To counteract Haley's First Law, one can obtain a "license" from the significant others. An employer who has been "tolerating" an alcoholic employee might find the request to license improvement in the alcoholic somewhat strange, since his motive has always been to help. However, when he is alerted, he may sometimes report difficulties he is having with the "new" person now working for him. Alerting relatives to the possibility that patients will go through "phases" in their treatment which might be difficult for the entire family has long been a technique for obtaining a license for patients to change. Family therapy is often important as a method for obtaining a license.

Negotiating a license is extremely important. The concept applies not only to the therapeutic situation but to many life events in which alteration of one individual's behavior may be perceived as threatening to other members of his group. I know of one black psychologist who feels he was given a "scholarship" by the gang on his street in Harlem when he was growing up. When others who had not negotiated a license to live "straight" attempted to do so, they were often framed by the gang, brought along unknowingly on an escapade that would get them into trouble, solely in order to oblige them to live the life of a gang member. Similar findings have been reported regarding the spread of drug addiction within networks, or, more innocuously, with respect to the nondrinker at a cocktail party. Departure from the shared behavior patterns is apt to meet with resistance, and to be unsuccessful unless the matter of permission is dealt with.

INDIRECT METHODS

Recently I saw a patient who had visited several previous therapists regarding her son. She did not like what they had to say to her, so she continued to search for one who would sympathize with her plight as she saw it. Her son was nineteen years old, living at home, and being babied by her, including cutting his meat at the table. She had done the same thing with two older daughters who had done very well, left the house, obtained honors in school, married, one of them finally producing a grandchild. It was the attention that she now devoted to the grandchild that seemed to trigger an angry response in her son, which in turn sent her to seek therapy. Every therapist in one way or another immediately attempted to separate the son from the household and implied that her approach to child rearing was faulty. However, she had seen her way work exceptionally well with her daughters and rejected the therapists' suggestions. She wanted a therapist who would see her son and calm him down so that everything could return to the way it was.

Particularly with noncompliant patients, the negotiation has to begin "with the problem the patient has selected to present." In the above case the patient put forward a proposal which was ignored and rejected out of hand by most therapists, and as a result the therapy was terminated almost before it began. Erickson (1959), who always uses an indirect method, emphasizes that a strategic therapist must "start where the patient is." A patient once came to him asking to be hypnotized, claiming that he could not sit down during the consultation, but had to pace the floor. Erickson did not object. Instead he suggested that the patient pace in one direction and then another until Erickson's suggestions were taken readily. The approach in this case was to make very slight modifications in stages. Erickson (1959) calls his method "utilization technique."

Palazzoli and Prata (1975) have reported that in the course of research on rapid treatment done by the Italian *Centro per lo Studio della Famiglia* (Family Studies Center), they and their colleagues discovered a kind of intervention *which must be applied early in treatment*. Basically it consists of approving of all observed behavior of the patient and his family, especially those behaviors that have traditionally been considered pathological.

The explanation offered for this unusual point of view stems from the idea of homeostasis (stable state). It is assumed that whatever the patient or family might be doing is the result of an attempt to achieve a stable state in the crisis situation that brought them to therapy. Any criticism with its implication that change is necessary will appear to increase the threat to homeostasis and, in effect, cause the family to form a "monolithic coalition in order to ward us off." Second, if the pathological behavior is generated by a need to maintain the cohesion and organization of the family, *the motive*, so to speak, is worthwhile even if the means are not. By being positive about what the family is doing one aligns oneself with these motives at a time when the family or the patient is most threatened. The patient or the family, as a result, give the therapist a greater license. Montalvo and Haley (1973) make the same point. Family therapists have developed the bad habit of routinely challenging the concept that the child has problems, and instead criticize the parents. The result is that one is left with defensive parents who find it hard to work with the therapist.

When parents are asked to attend a family session because of the problems that their child is having, they feel very guilty. They secretly fear and expect that they will be criticized. In the last century one could have several children, some who "turned out well" and some who did not. More recently our culture gives the credit and the blame to parents for the behavior of their children. Any criticism will produce a defense of some variety, even if it is of the depressive sort which can effectively reduce a therapist to impotence just as well as any other defense. Parents are concerned with whether they are to be judged as good or bad. This "good mother, bad mother" issue was probably foremost in the mind of the patient described at the outset of this section.

Palazzoli (1974) points out that many children are extremely skillful in presenting their parents in the worst possible light. She has had extensive experience with anorexia patients who often manage to incite their parents to act in ways that are bound to be disapproved of by others, particularly therapists. This is a trap. In one of her cases the patient brought the discussion around to the premorbid phase of her life and managed to get her parents to express their antiquated views on sex, which showed them to be repressive and determined to thwart their daughter's nascent sexuality. In this case the therapists, rather than swallowing the bait and jumping on the parents, spoke of the parents' "obvious fascination with their daughter's feminine charms, and of the way in which they had succeeded in driving these charms home to the patient herself. They would certainly not have acted in the way they did had they thought her anything but highly desirable. In fact their assessment of the situation was one with which the patient must have been in full agreement. Why else had she always been so loyal to them and never used even the slightest subterfuge to defy their prohibitions?" (Palazzoli 1974, p. 229).

Palazzoli calls this the "positive connotation technique," and further points out that it is necessary to put all members of a family on the same plane. It is important to notice in the above quote how both the parents and the patient were dealt with in the same remark. By not taking sides, or appearing not to, the therapist is in a better position in relation to a family. He is, in a sense, superordinate to them, above them, in such a fashion that he is better able to influence the process within the family. Palazzoli refers to the positive connotation as the "golden road for entering, and being freely admitted into, the family system."

I have sometimes referred to what Palazzoli calls the "positive connotation technique" as the "dumb psychiatrist approach." In this method the psychiatrist just doesn't seem to catch on to what the patient is trying to say. The patient may enter therapy by complaining about his parents (whether or not they are present in the therapy session). The "dumb psychiatrist" persistently fails to grasp what the patient is trying to say by always assuming a positive connotation. If the problem is that a parent is complaining about a child, the therapist "fails" to understand that, too.

Starting where the patient is, the positive connotation, the good parent, bad parent issue, and the dumb psychiatrist approach all describe initial postures that facilitate negotiations with the patient who is noncompliant. They are varieties of indirect methods. It is sometimes easier to utilize such a method if the therapist has a theory about why the more direct approach will not work. Palazzoli's explanation regarding the homeostatic reactions of systems is helpful in a general fashion. I would suggest several less general explanations which are not contradictory to hers but are on a lower level of theorizing.

CHANGING THE CONTEXT

Attitudes about an event or an act may be influenced as much by the framework in which it is perceived as by the act or event itself. One method of influencing a patient's attitude about an act is to redefine or modify its context. For example, prescription of a medication, particularly a major tranquilizer, may be construed by the patient to mean that he is sick or crazy. Although he may not object to the actual act of taking a pill, he might react negatively to the context which places him with stigmatized people. If we assume there is no leeway regarding the prescription itself, that the medication is necessary, then we can modify the context in which it is seen. This can be accomplished by offering an alternative explanation for the cause of the patient's problem. We can state that about 10 percent of the population seems to have a genetic tendency to develop a chemical imbalance under stress and that this can be corrected by pills, just as a vitamin deficiency can be corrected by pills. By placing psychotropic medication in the same context as vitamins, the patient's willingness to take the medication may be enhanced.

In this section's initial illustration, in which the mother wanted her son to be given medication or otherwise persuaded to remain at home, all the professionals she consulted were critical of her. If a therapist were to emphasize instead what a conscientious mother she was, he might at some point be able to suggest that it was a mistake to reward such an ingrate of a son as she was doing. Instead, he should be given a chance to see for himself how valuable her love was. In other words, she should

kick him out of the house if he continued to behave objectionably.

We have been discussing methods of promoting compliance
by adjusting the context of behavior. The same approach can
also be employed to eliminate or change a patient's actions. For
example, a hostile wife's lack of sexual response to her husband
can be placed in another context: that she is actually being very
nice to protect him from her intense sexuality, which she fears
will be too much for him. Within this framework, hostility would
have to be expressed in sexual responsiveness (Watzlawick,
Weakland, and Fisch 1974). In short, although it may appear
initially to be objectionably manipulative, this method of modifying contexts while approving content is often an effective way
of dealing with patients who are reluctant to cooperate with
therapeutic strategies. When Palazzoli "approves" of the parents'
old-fashioned, repressive sexual mores, she places them within
the context of fascination with the daughter's sexiness. This subject is discussed again as "reframing" in chapter 5.

INDIRECT MESSAGES

A suggestion delivered as an aside allows the patient to
decide whether or not to accept it. If he rejects it, he is not turning down the therapist. If he accepts, he is doing so on the basis
of his own wishes. This probably applies to an interpretation as
well as a prescription. Psychoanalysts have developed a style of
musing ("I was wondering to myself whether it might be possible that there is a connection between X and Y?") that is often
highly effective in communicating their point of view. There is
little a patient can say about a musing remark. He cannot say it
is wrong since it was presented as an aside, merely an idle
thought. It is as if the therapist were thinking aloud, giving the
patient the option of accepting the communication without
having to confront the therapist if he does not wish to do so.

A patient once came to see me with the complaint that she
could have an orgasm only when she imagined that she was

being spanked, preferably by her mother. She would begin to have the fantasy as soon as her husband made sexual advances toward her. I wondered aloud what would happen if she waited a while before she began having her fantasy. She returned the next week to tell me that she had followed my "advice" with success. At first I didn't know what she meant, since in my mind I had given her no advice. As she continued talking, I realized that my musing question had been accepted as a directive. Experience suggests that this is probably the most effective means of delivering a suggestion to certain patients.

COERCION AND AVERSIVE METHODS

A crisis is a fear-producing situation which mobilizes patients; coercion is a fear-producing or disagreeable situation created by a therapist. Coercion that is induced by a therapist is one of the prime sources of symptom substitution (see chapter 7). However, coercion can work in some cases where the therapist suggests a punishment for a symptom. For example, a patient's fee can be made to depend upon how much weight the patient loses. I have known therapists to raise their fees when they discover how much money a patient is squandering on drugs or some other expensive problem. Coercion has been a fairly common strategy in therapeutic efforts to cure anorexia nervosa. Typically, the recalcitrant eater is confined to bed in a tiny, unadorned cubicle with nothing to do, and must gain a specified amount of weight in order to be allowed to walk around, leave the room, have social contacts, or engage in ordinary activities. While this method almost always works in the short run (and I might add it is attempted only with patients whose dieting is approaching a life-endangering level), it may be perceived by the patient as a humiliating and grossly coercive experience, with unfortunate subsequent results that have been known to include suicide (Bruch 1974).

More sophisticated, and probably more effective, coercion strategies link a virtuous but unpopular task (such as studying, if the patient is a student) with the behavior one wishes to extinguish. Every time the patient displays the symptom, he must also perform the specified task. For example, Erickson (in Haley 1973a, chap. 6) has treated nocturnal enuresis by requiring the patient to get up at 3:00 A.M. and practice penmanship with his mother. In reference to this strategy, Haley (1973b) has pointed out that the overinvolvement between mother and son was really what was being punished. Such rather humorous strategies, in which the patient himself sometimes sees the humor, are quite different from the crude coercion used with anorexics. It is one thing to say "I have a crazy idea which might just work," and another to compel a patient to relinquish a symptom.

A young student came to see me complaining that almost everything reminded her of the good times she used to have as a child with her father. She might see a father and child on the bus or merely see someone who looked kindly. She would become gloomy on these occasions and her schoolwork would suffer. I suggested *with her consent* that, whenever she experienced these feelings, she go to the library and study for two hours. Although she thought that she might not be able to study, she did agree to go to the library and sit with her books in front of her. The result was that she quickly extinguished her bouts of sadness and got straight A's.

Another patient in her late twenties was referred to me with a totally disorganized life. She never got anywhere on time, had quit her job as a schoolteacher, and squandered her inheritance on an ill-conceived plan in show business. She described herself as "spaced out, unable to get my things together." Quite by accident she obtained a job working part time for a physician who was even more disturbed than herself, but in another direction. Apparently he took amphetamines regularly, was involved in a rather odd medical practice, and, most importantly, lost his temper violently at the slightest disturbance. He so frightened her that she became much better organized. If she did not come in on time, he became so angry that she did everything in her power to arrive at his office punctually. If she was "foggy and spaced out," he flew into a violent rage. For some reason that I was never able to determine, she did not leave his employment when he became enraged at her. I suspect that her very "fogginess" itself protected her somewhat from his onslaughts. Both of them seemed to know that they were good for each other. He knew that few people could put up with him, and she knew that she was benefiting from the experience. Eventually they became somewhat friendly. He would occasionally invite her to spend the weekend with his family at their country house, and she would do various errands for his mother. I believe that this relationship was probably the most therapeutic experience that the patient had, yet I would classify it as a coercion experience.

CONFUSION

Several investigators have reported that confusion on the part of the patient enhances a therapist's influence. For a patient who doesn't know what to expect in a therapeutic situation, the general attitude and silence of the typical therapist might be unsettling; the patient doesn't know what is expected of him or what he should anticipate from the therapist. Some therapists seek actively to heighten such confusion in their patients in order to increase their own influence. Such efforts can be called "crisis mongering." Thus a therapist might seem to make little sense in what he says and does in therapy, leaving the patient unclear about how he should act in order to obtain praise. A similar technique has been used by Erickson to induce hypnosis. Erickson (1964b) claims to have thought of this idea when he and another man collided in the street on a rainy day. Erickson looked at his watch and said that it was exactly ten minutes of two, although it was closer to 4:00 P.M. He did this with elaborate courtesy before the other man had a chance to recover his poise; then he walked on. About a half a block away he turned around and saw his victim still turning back every now and then to glance at him. As in a hypnotic induction procedure, his attention had been totally fixed on Erickson. In a sense, he was in a trance. People who are thus manipulated are eager for some information that is understandable. They are likely to accept the first clear directive they can get just to be able to clear up their confusion.

Therapists confuse patients with interpretations, with questions about seemingly irrelevant things, even with odd behavior such as lying down on the floor during the session. Technically, such confusion must be followed by a very clear and distinct request; presumably, the patient will be so happy to understand this proposal that he will perform it readily. If the request is not clear, however, the patient will be further confused.

FLATTERY

Finally, warm, flattering remarks, "ingratiation tactics," or "the power of friendship" have been proposed as effective motivators. Emphasizing similarities between the patient and the therapist, expressing a liking for the patient, and noting the patient's most positive attributes in a noncompetitive manner have been mentioned. After confiding in a therapist, many patients naturally develop a fondness for him and think of him as a friend. This friendship exerts a certain power over a patient, who, in order to keep the friendship, is likely to follow prescriptions. Gillis (1974) reports a therapist who found that the most helpful technique he had developed was to say to patients, after friendship had been built up, that he was afraid that he was not helping them enough. Patients were quick to reassure him that he was helping them and that they were, just this week, planning to try out some of the suggestions he had made.

CHAPTER 4

Hypnosis: The Ceremonial Aspects of Healing

AT ONE POINT early in his career, Rachmaninoff found himself unable to write music. He was hypnotized by a Moscow psychiatrist who each day repeated the same verbal formula to him as he lay half asleep in an armchair: "You will work with great facility. . . . The concerto will be of excellent quality. . . ." The incantation, always the same and without interruption, resulted in an unqualified success. Rachmaninoff wrote his Second Piano Concerto, whose third movement has been popularized in the song, "Full Moon and Empty Arms." This concerto, said to be the most frequently performed in the entire piano repertoire, is dedicated to the psychiatrist, Dr. Dahl.

Dahl's strategy entailed the use of a direct injunction or "suggestion" while Rachmaninoff was in a relaxed state. Often hypnosis is associated with relaxation and might be more properly categorized as merely another means of relaxing someone. However, there is bound to be some controversy about whether the disparate strategies related to or associated with hypnosis can be grouped in any one category. For example, while hypnosis is most often associated with relaxation, it has also been connected with a hyperalert state. In fact, defining hypnosis empirically is difficult, so that categorizing it anywhere has its problems. It has long been hoped that some physiological sign of hypnosis will persist against the various backgrounds presented by hypnotic behavior, but the possibilities seem remote at this time. At present hypnosis does not represent an explanation of behavior but must be considered a term applied to a complex, somewhat distinctive relationship between patient and therapist, often involving some sort of relaxation and some distortion of reality or inability to be distracted. Certain investigators would include so-called nonvolitional behavior, such as an arm floating upward without the patient's making it do so (an obvious impossibility which will be discussed in chapter 6 under the term "Counterwill"). Since such behavior (relaxation, the arm floating, etc.) can come about for many reasons (for example, merely the desire to please), it seems most appropriate to define hypnosis as the *situation* in which the hypnotic *ceremony* takes place, without assigning any necessary behavior to the subject.

Ceremonial healing is as significant in psychiatry as any other area of medicine. Hypnosis is the most commonly used brief treatment ceremony in psychiatry. When it is successful, it can be brilliantly so. Therefore it is often useful to obtain some idea of the patient's ability, attitude, and strategic capacity to accept the ceremonial situation, to concentrate, and to use his imagination. Such a brief test takes only between five and fifteen minutes. It also will give the therapist some notion about the style of psychotherapy that will be best suited to the patient. Some patients do not accept or react badly to the classical psychoanalytic technique of silence, ambiguity, and lack of structure (although that mode is often selected out of respect for the patient's abilities), and prefer the more direct, structured style of hypnosis.

Hypnotic techniques almost always incorporate an additional strategy, which in many cases could be used independently of hypnosis. For example, the treatment of phobias can be achieved by extended exposure to the frightening situation. It really doesn't matter how that exposure is achieved. If a hypnotist induces a trance, presents the patient with an amulet which he endows with special magical characteristics, and then sends the patient out to expose himself to the frightening situation (to purchase a dog if he has a dog phobia), he is actually using an exposure strategy within the ceremonial context of hypnosis. If he has another patient induce a "self-hypnotic state" ten times a day and repeat some verbal formula to himself ("Cigarettes are poison. If I want to live, I must have a healthy body. I owe myself this protection"), in addition to a hypnotic ceremony he is using an "affirmation," a technique that has its origins in prayer (Spiegel 1970).

Hypnosis can stand on its own as an effective ceremony that makes people feel better and often improves symptoms and problem situations. However, hypnosis naturally leads the therapist to search for something more he can do besides providing a healing ceremony, for what to do once the patient is hypnotized, what additional strategy to incorporate in the trance. For these reasons hypnosis is an excellent way to begin to learn about strategic therapy. It is both an opening ceremony and a transition to a midgame strategy.

THE ORIGINS OF HYPNOSIS

Hypnosis was derived from those religious healing ceremonies that were "popular" or, more precisely, consistent with the belief systems preceding it. As exorcism declined in Europe, the forerunners of hypnotic ceremonies were developing to take its place. In 1775 an honest, sincere, and modest country priest with a great natural talent for the treatment of disorders by exorcism was induced to pit his powers against an insincere, ambitious, and prideful "scientist" named Mesmer. The neverending series of cures that the country priest had produced with "religious faith," as he called his central method, had been a great embarrassment in the intellectual climate of the Age of Enlightenment. Sick patients had been brought before him and commanded in the name of God, that is, their demon or incubus was commanded, to communicate with the priest. If this didn't occur, if the patient made no sign, he was referred to ordinary physicians. If a sign was forthcoming a monumental battle between priest and incubus occurred. The method was nonintellectual, mystical, and mysterious, but its success was well documented by the very scientists who found the whole idea so abhorrent.

The scientist against whom the priest was pitted argued in essence that he could do with his science all that an exorcist could do with his religion, and apparently he proved his case. He claimed that magnetism was responsible for the effect he demonstrated, which he called "animal magnetism." The scientist had written his dissertation on the subject and, as we now know, plagarized it from an earlier source. Nevertheless, the country priest was effectively defeated and sent back to his parish with the stipulation from Rome to accept only screened referrals from a specific religious source, while the scientist went on to found a career based on the phenomenon of animal magnetism, which came eventually to be named "Mesmerism." There is an irony in the confrontation of these two men, one an honest exorcist of immense talent and the other an opportunist. Mesmer is said to have been jealous all his life of the priest's ability. The difference probably had to do with the priest's belief in himself and his religion, having cured himself of certain maladies with religious faith. It is hard to imagine Mesmer as a true believer or without doubts about his practices.

While Gassner, the priest, is all but forgotten, Mesmer became famous and went on to found an institute in Paris which was eventually investigated by a commission, appointed by the French crown, composed of Benjamin Franklin, Lavoiser, Guillotine, and others. The commission rejected Mesmer's magnetism explanation and concluded that all they witnessed could be explained by the imagination. They were more than a little bit critical of Mesmer's seductive "induction" techniques (which will be discussed later.)

Ultimately the most significant action that Mesmer took was to train (for a high fee) the Marquis de Puseygur, a French aristocrat, who practiced Mesmerism without charge on his estates, principally beneath a huge tree that survived until 1944. (When it fell in a storm, it was carried off in little pieces as talismans by the local peasants.) What was significant about Puseygur's practice was that a servant of his, Victor Race, went into a trance that was different from that which Mesmer usually produced. Race's trance was sleeplike.* Furthermore, during the trance state Race explained to the Marquis how best to put him into that sort of a trance, and for the first time told him that hypnotized subjects were compliant to commands. He remembered nothing afterward. Sleepwalking was exceedingly popular as a human interest subject at that time. One heard stories about people amnestically walking across the rooftops of Paris who might fall from their precarious perches if their names were called and they woke up. Victor Race apparently incorporated this popular concern into his personal schema of a trance. This type of trance had probably been noticed before, but Puseygur saw in it important possibilities.

The classic Mesmeric trance—what people did when they were Mesmerized—resembled what people did when Gassner, the country priest, used his method of exorcism. They went into something that might be called an attack or "crisis." † This is apparently a very old model for a healing ceremony, seen today

---

* This fact has prompted Eysenck (1957) to nominate Puseygur and Race as the inventors of hypnosis. This is a distinct minority opinion, but I think it has merit. Mesmer developed the first popular quasi-scientific healing cult or human potential sect, the modern representatives of which include, for example, Scientology. Many of these sects use methods encompassing a core of psychologically effective techniques, as was the case with Mesmer.

† Not to be confused with the current meaning of the term; here it is synonymous with "attack."

among certain Latin subjects. In Puerto Rican New Yorkers one can observe an *ataque*, an excited state somewhat like an epileptic fit (which may have been the original point of departure for the attack type of trance, as sleepwalking was the model for the sleeplike trance). An illustration of a Mesmeric crisis is provided in the recorded testimonial of Charles de Hussey, a Major of Infantry and Knight of the Royal Military Order of St. Louis, who swore publicly to this statement:

After four years of useless treatment by other doctors, I consulted Mesmer. My head was constantly shaking and my neck was bent forward. My eyes protruded and were considerably inflamed. My back was almost completely paralysed and I could only speak with difficulty . . . (Eysenck 1957, p. 26).

De Hussey was treated by Mesmer and experienced a series of crises: "ice coming from my limbs, followed by great heat and foetid perspiration." He ends his sworn statement with "Now after four months, I am completely cured."

The Mesmeric attack model of hypnosis gave way to the Puseygur–Race sleep model. Braid, a Scottish physician, later coined the term "nervous sleep" or "hypnosis." Although there is no evidence that hypnosis is similar to sleep, the interaction between sleep and hypnosis is still of research interest, especially in the area of dream research. Up to 10 percent of subjects hypnotized have little or no memory of what occurred during the trance. Since one does not have much memory of what happened during one's sleep, the coincidence supports the sleep model. However, in hypnosis this amnesia is not spontaneous. Subjects who do not expect to have an amnesia do not forget what occurred during hypnosis. Some subjects, of course, expect amnesia from what they have heard or read, and others are specifically told they will forget (Hilgard and Cooper 1965; Cooper 1966). Some forgetting seems to be the normal failure to remember every detail and cannot be reversed, but the amnesia that occurs by suggestion can be reversed by hypnotizing a subject again.

In very recent years the Puseygur–Race model of a hypnotic trance has once again been revised. In this more modern model of hypnosis the emphasis is not on sleep, and "falling into a deep sleep" is not part of the hypnotist's patter. What one speaks of is "deep relaxation." This model has the advantage of increasing the range of hypnosis to somewhere between 70 and 80 percent of those who come for psychotherapy. However, it is important to emphasize that the criteria for hypnosis are different in this model than in the sleep model. Distortion of reality and inability to be distracted are less important as prerequisites. In this model one speaks of relaxing completely, of getting a feeling of floating pleasantly, and so on.

Members of the French commission appointed to investigate Mesmer's claims dismissed his animal magnetism theory and substituted one of their own. They suggested that Mesmerism was entirely explicable in terms of the powers of the imagination. Furthermore, they were not impressed with the behavioral feats of those who were Mesmerized. This may have been due to the fact that by this time Mesmer himself had drifted from a clinical focus to what we would today call a "growth experience" goal. At this period in his career, wealthy and probably predominantly healthy Parisians came to his salon in order to have "an experience." Mesmer appeared in flowing purple robes with soft music in the background and worked with large groups and gimmicky equipment. Then, as today, such effects depend heavily upon the imagination.

IMAGINATION AND TRANCE

"Imagination" is the ability to form a mental concept of something that is not actually presented to the senses. "Imagery" is the visual (or other type) of representation thus produced. "A trance" can be defined as a contraction of peripheral awareness and an increase in focal awareness. This state of intense concentration or absorption excludes the usual clues used in reality testing. Anyone who is capable of a high degree of imagination must be absorbed in it and therefore to some extent in a trance, but the concept of a trance goes beyond intense concentration on imagery to include concentration on anything.

In a trance one can be absorbed in something that is imaginary or real. One can even be "entranced" while shooting a rifle, as Sullivan (1956, p. 39) once observed. He reported sticking a pin in a companion's buttocks while his friend was concentrating on a target. His companion had so contracted his field of attention that he felt nothing. In this case the trance had nothing to do with the imagination. On the other hand, Spock (1957, p. 315) cautions parents about roughhousing with their children and introducing a fantasy element ("I'm a bear and I'm going to get you") because the child is likely to believe, for the moment, that you actually are a bear. Here the absorption is in an imaginary element. Accompanying the absorption is a degree of reality distortion and suspension of disbelief such as adults experience in the theatre or movies. When the curtain comes down and the lights go on, there is frequently a short pause before the applause while members of the audience relinquish their trance. Freud pointed out the relationship between hypnosis and being in love. There is a degree of imagination, trance, and suspension of reality testing in both.

When a trance occurs ceremoniously (whether involving imagination or not), we often refer to it as hypnosis. It is also possible merely to ask a subject to imagine something intensely and produce a trance without any ceremony. In this case it is a good idea to start with something nonthreatening in which the contrasts are strong, such as entering a pleasant, dimly lit room, and then exiting into bright sunlight. From this point one could proceed to more complex imagery or even to a strategy usually reserved for hypnosis.

Some investigators, notably Erickson, feel that they can identify subjects who are so engrossed in the opening phases of therapy that they have fallen into a spontaneous trance state. Barber (1969) is critical of Erickson's equation of this sort of trance with the hypnotically induced type, but there seem to be therapists who prefer the ceremonial induction and those whose strategies are quite similar (i.e., direct suggestion) who find the ceremonies unnecessary.

The depth of a trance varies with the context and the subject. For example, the same person who can become so absorbed in a newspaper that he does not hear himself addressed can find motion pictures not conducive to total involvement.

IMAGINATION AND HYPNOSIS

Hypnosis is related to imagery in a complex way. One approach to the unraveling of their relationship is to expand the formulation of J. R. Hilgard (1974) that the success of hypnosis has an *ability* component and an *attitudinal* component, by adding a *strategic* component as a third major dimension.

Attitudinal Component. Apprehension about novelty, unwillingness to accept the hypnotist-subject relationship, and fear of loss of control interfere with hypnosis. Curiosity, a liking for the novel, and willingness to assume an attitude of passive concentration and to accept the hypnotist as a teacher and guide favor hypnosis.

Ability Component. The ability component of hypnosis is thought to be the capacity of the subject to use his imagination. This often originates in early childhood in total involvement in books, dramatic play, religion, imaginary companions, daydreaming, and the savoring of sensory experiences.

In the past five years several investigators have suggested that subjects who are more visual and imaginative use the nondominant side of the brain. The left (dominant) side of the brain is thought to process information in a verbal, quantitative fashion, and the right side in a visual-spatial manner. When a subject is asked by someone seated in front of him, looking him in the eye, to solve a problem, the subject will often divert his eyes to one side or the other. These eye movements are activated by the opposite brain hemisphere. Thus if a subject looks to the right, the movement is controlled by the left side of the brain. People whose left brain hemisphere is dominant think in more logical, verbal terms. People whose right brain hemisphere is dominant have been reported to be more visual, imaginative, to daydream more, and to be more susceptible to hypnosis (Bakan 1969).

Another ability component of hypnosis involves the capacity to maintain intense concentration over a long period of time. Among other factors, distractibility can result from the pressure of other thoughts besides that which the hypnotist is suggesting, or from a malignant cognitive process such as schizophrenia. It is therefore difficult to use a hypnotic strategy with a schizophrenic.

Strategic Component. Spanos (1971) has shown that some patients who are able to demonstrate behavior that is "not volitional" (such as an arm floating upward) do so by using an image that helps the act to take place (e.g., a balloon is imagined tied to the arm, causing it to float upward). If such a patient can become absorbed in this imagination, his arm appears to him to float upward without his making it do so.

Such strategic components of hypnotic behavior are usually hinted at by the hypnotist in his patter. He is likely to say, "Your arm is light and buoyant like a balloon." In inducing eyelid closure he might say, "Your eyelids are heavy, heavy as lead, weighted with lead," which the subject can then utilize imaginatively. Sometimes subjects create their own images spontaneously. Spanos reports one subject whose arm floated upward as he imagined that it was hollow and someone was pumping air into it.

Spanos refers to this as "goal-directed fantasy," and his work suggests that subjects who report nonvolitional acts while under hypnosis employ their ability to imagine in this particular way. For example, a subject asked to forget the number four tried very hard to do so, but the more that she tried the more she actually thought about it. (See chapter 6, "Reverse Psychology.") Other subjects who were able to have an amnesia for the number four consistently reported the occurrence of an imaginary event which produced the disappearance of the visualized number. They might imagine the numbers one through ten on a blackboard, with an erased space for the number four, or children's blocks with numbers on them but with a blank space in the series where the block with four belongs.

At present there is a controversy about the place of imagery in psychotherapy. Psychoanalysts, after an initial period of using images, decided that images are defensive interruptions of the main flow of verbal ideas and are motivated by resistance. In this approach images are to be analyzed away. A second point of view, mostly European in origin, takes the position that images are an expression of underlying impulses and not defenses against them. The former point of view concentrates on interpreting the images, finding what they conceal, while the latter point of view concentrates on what they reveal, developing these images for further, sometimes guided, expression. There is even a controversy about whether images or verbal reports are more accurate data. Those who favor images tend to feel that verbal reports can be clichés that have been thought out carefully before—what in Alcoholics Anonymous has been termed "playing one's tapes." As such they are not thought to be useful. Singer (1971) has gone so far as to suggest that there is an association between being able to produce images and the ability to have fun, live imaginatively, discriminate between fantasy and reality, and be less disconcerted by unexpected thoughts and images.

Some of the controversy about imagery is dispelled by the

concept of right- and left-brained dominance. Whether or not this actually turns out to be a valid anatomical distinction, there do appear to be two distinct styles. One is verbal, logical, and cognitive, which is compatible with the psychoanalytic method. The other style is more visual, intuitive, and creative, for which a procedure using imagery is more appropriate. Spiegel (1974) has reported that a determination of where a patient fits in this classification is essential to the therapeutic outcome. A "right-brained" patient whose style is more suited to guided imagery—whether using hypnosis or not—can react badly to a treatment strategy that removes guidelines and allows too free a rein. Such patients seek direction from the therapist; they may become confused and sometimes severely upset if none is provided.

A distinct European school began with the experiments of E. Caslant in the 1920s. Caslant, a physicist, began experimenting with subjects by asking them to imagine themselves rising up into space, and to observe their ease or difficulty in so doing. If they imagined obstacles (such as a net) he would suggest various sources to overcome the obstacle ("use a sword to cut through that web"). He was mainly interested in clairvoyance and other extrasensory abilities. Desoille, an engineer, was a student of Caslant who continued to study some of these phenomena, but his study developed into a psychotherapeutic practice. He developed the technique of the *rêve evielle,* "the directed daydream." A Sorbonne professor, Gaston Bachelard, popularized Desoille's work. Singer (1971) has compared the influence of the use of directed imagery in Europe to the influence of psychoanalysis in the United States.

Ferenczi and Jung had also used something like the directed daydream. Jung called his technique *active imagination.* It seemed to offer him material to analyze, and to show his patients, most of whom were unimaginative but successful businessmen, a way to enliven their lives. Ferenczi asked his patients to "fabricate" fantasies and would occasionally prime the pump by offering them examples of possible fantasies until they were able to continue on their own. These *forced fantasies* of Ferenczi and the active imagination of Jung were mainly used in what might be called the American way to discover what was behind them. The European method was to assume that such fantasies were important and meaningful in themselves for the patient, that the process of having them (of cutting through the web blocking one from rising) was itself beneficial. Leuner in Germany, Desoille in France, Assagioli in Italy have employed imagery in the latter fashion. Hammer (1967) has introduced these methods in the United States. The experience of the image is considered therapeutic and insight is used adjunctively. Hammer suggests that certain scenes be suggested to the patient: being in a meadow, a house, a cave, a forest, and climbing a mountain. Another technique is to "strengthen the ego" by a symbolic confrontation, for example between the patient and a large snake which he stares down until it is transformed into a mammal and then finally a person. If the final person is a mother figure, the suggestion is that the original conflict was with the patient's mother.

The European approach has been detailed by Shorr. Shorr's book (1974) contains an extensive series of suggestions for tasks that can be given to a patient who is capable of using his imagination. It does not necessarily follow that the patient should be hypnotized, but J. R. Hilgard's previously mentioned work (1974) suggests that such a patient would probably be a good hypnotic subject—that is, the patient would have the ability component of hypnosis. Shorr classifies the types of imagery into some of the following categories: *Dual imagery* is the technique of asking a subject to imagine two different things, in the hope that in this way a conflict can be expressed. For example, the subject or patient is asked to imagine two objects, two animals, two forces acting on him, two containers, or a word on the front and a word on the back of him. In using *sexual imagery,* a patient is asked to imagine that he is entering a room with a hole in the floor into which he looks. *Body imagery* involves asking a patient what part of his body is his core, the residence of his anger (or other emotion). A classic body image task is to imagine taking a trip through one's own body. *Cathartic imagery* is usually accomplished by asking a patient to imagine a person and then an "impossible scream" (what would be the most difficult thing to scream at [tell] the other person.) Shorr also suggests several ways of focusing what the patient imagines: asking him to complete sentences like "I am not . . . ," "How dare you . . . ," "I am . . . ," "Never refer to me as . . . ," and so on; asking most/least questions (what is the most difficult thing to say, the least difficult, and so on) and inquiring how a particular image relates to the patient's life.

A patient was troubled by what happened to her during a drug-induced "bad trip" in which she saw the witch from *Snow White and the Seven Dwarfs,* who told her that people are forced to commit suicide. This patient had a fairly well-adjusted life but was troubled by this fantasy. Such a patient might be helped by a guided daydream in which she has less uncontrolled fantasies about the witch. One can develop a hierarchy of possible guided daydreams which slowly get the fantasy under control. Start by just suggesting that the witch is at a distance and move on to a fairly pleasant transaction with her, such as giving her a glass of water to quench her thirst. It is contraindicated to suggest a violent destruction of the fantasy, since in clinical experience this creates anxiety, presumably because the witch is an externalized part of the patient. This technique has been used with people troubled by recurrent nightmares.

Freud's original use of images was to ask the patient to lie on the couch as Freud pressed on the patient's forehead or temples while counting to five. The patient was told that he would have an image related to his problem. Freud became so sure of himself and his method that even if his patients claimed that no image, idea, word, or thought occurred to them, he would still insist that they were censoring something. It is still a helpful self-confrontation technique. However, used as Freud apparently did, without preliminary imagery tasks, there is likely to be considerable blocking.

A twenty-one-year-old patient came to see me with a wide array of physical complaints which, after approximately $1,000 worth of medical expenses, had not proven amenable to any diagnosis. She had gone away to another state with her twenty-year-old boyfriend but had become ill there. Her numerous symptoms required her to return home. When I spoke to her, she denied any knowledge of what her problem was. When the Freud technique was used, her first thought was "mother." Following this she could speak about her fear of leaving her parents and had a symptom-free week.

In the Human Potential Movement imagery is used to create intense emotional experiences. For example, here is one "exercise" using the cathartic method:

Get on your knees on the floor, and grasp one end of a towel with both hands, as if you were clutching the tail of a rattlesnake. From the pit of your stomach work up a paroxsym of fear, loathing, and anger. Remember that if you ease up the snake can whip around and bite you. Close your eyes, breathe deeply—and smash it down as hard as you can; keep thrashing until you kill it. You are likely to experience a great feeling of relief and expansion (Lewis and Streitfeld 1972, p. 151).

In such examples we have come full circle back to Mesmer's original performances, which gave his subject the opportunity for an experience.

HYPNOTIC INDUCTION

A trance can occur spontaneously, as in the theatre, and also under ceremonial circumstances. In the latter case, one speaks of "hypnosis" as being "induced." Hypnosis can be induced by a hypnotist or by the subject, in which case it is called "self-hypnosis." Barber (Barber and Calverley 1964) has argued that urging and encouragement can elicit all the phenomena of hypnosis without the induction ceremony. In his experimental studies he has informed subjects that "*everyone* can do this if they really try. I myself can do this quite easily and *all* the previous subjects that participated in the experiment were able to do it" (Barber and Calverley 1964, p. 586). In this way he has been able to elicit from his subjects such behavior as hallucinations, anesthesia, and age regression.

Hypnotized subjects are not usually subjected to as much pressure for compliance as in Barber's experiments. His work has led to a "state" versus "trait" controversy that has been reviewed by Hilgard (1975). Clinically, the issue is whether the subject (his traits) or the hypnotist (the state induced) is most responsible for the trance. Spiegel (1972), a proponent of the former view, believes that the patient has a "trance capacity" which he is taught to tap by the hypnotist. There is a heuristic value for a beginning hypnotist in adopting this view. Other clinicians suggest that the skill of the hypnotist influences the subject's responses. This is closely related to the question of modification of hypnotizability. Diamond (1974) has reviewed the experimental literature related to this issue.

Shor (Shor and Cobb 1968) has pointed out that the question of state versus trait is clouded by the fact that experimental laboratory conditions seldom resemble clinical experience, since experimental designs rely on standard induction procedures in a specified context, while clinicians are free to apply a variety of methods and to modify procedures, timing, and other dimensions of the experience in intuitive and adaptive ways. For example, Erickson (1952, p. 21) has reported a case in which his procedure consisted of first failing completely to induct the patient since the patient, a medical student, was determined to defeat him. He then got complete cooperation for an "illustration of the imagination" which was, in fact, a trance. Such craft is not taken into account in standard research protocols.

Regardless of such considerations as personal cunning and resourcefulness on the part of the hypnotist, the successful outcome of a hypnotic strategy often depends on the "pitch," not the induction or the depth of trance. The more numerous and varied the metaphors used with a patient *after the induction* to achieve an aim, the more likely the strategy is to succeed. For example, Spiegel's (1970) widely heralded hypnotic treatment for smoking does not depend upon the ease or depth of induction so much as upon the subsequent pitch, which includes repetition, varied media, vivid metaphors, and an emphasis on health.

There is a plateau of susceptibility beyond which it is difficult, and for most clinicians not worthwhile, to attempt to elicit hypnotic behavior. Depth of trance often has little to do with the patient's ability to utilize a postinduction strategy unless one is hoping to use a phenomenon specific to hypnosis, such as age regression. There are conflicting opinions about attempting to deepen trances, which may result from failure to distinguish between depth of trance and the patient's successful use of a postinduction strategy. Drugs which sedate the patient do not enhance hypnotic capacity since they dull the patient's abilities. Stimulants may be of some value. Drugs widely used to alter states of consciousness do not assist hypnosis.

Depth of trance can be measured. The Sarbin Scale (see Appendix C)* is both a representation of a sleep model of hypnosis and an index of trance susceptibility. In teaching hypnosis I suggest that the clinician, without fanfare, read the Sarbin protocol to a patient, as the instructions indicate, while having him stare at a spot rather than a light, and then introduce whatever hypnotic strategy was planned.

* The Stanford Scale (Weitzenhoffer and Hilgard 1959) is a modernized and more detailed version of this protocol which can profitably be consulted.

Another scale with accompanying induction method is offered by Spiegel (1973). It uses relaxation and concentration as its basic model, and emphasizes the extent of upward eye roll (1972) as an index of trance capacity.

As Spiegel points out, there are three different categories of trance induction: the clinical induction, fear, and seduction. Police interrogation depends on fear and occasionally produces a false confession that is based on hypnotic compliance. The Svengali-like seductive control developed in certain sadomasochistic relationships (as in the Manson "family") also seems to resemble hypnosis and is often seen in psychiatric practice (moreso, at any rate, than are fear-induced states).

The clinical induction of hypnosis can be divided into three stages. First, the hypnotist must develop his influence. This stage is approximately equivalent to the subject matter of the opening in strategic psychotherapy, but in hypnosis there has always tended to be an emphasis on flamboyant behavior. Mesmer, for instance, appeared in flowing purple robes and with a background of music. It does not seem necessary to be flamboyant today. As discussed in previous chapters, there are many ways to impress a subject. The point worth stressing, however, is that, no matter how it is done, control of the patient's expectations is essential.

The second stage of induction is providing a "linking maneuver." Here some involuntary action appears to come about as a result of the hypnotist's command. For example, "You will feel tired and sleepy when you close your eyes" (while listening to the drone of the hypnotist's patter) is a statement that is likely to be true of most subjects who have had a busy day and who have rushed to get to the appointment with the hypnotist. While subjects are not usually aware of the degree of their fatigue, they suddenly recognize it when they close their eyes. What is important, though, is that they *link* their tiredness to the command of the hypnotist.

All induction techniques depend on a natural physiological

response which the patient does not realize is a natural response. Thus, in the induction technique in which the patient stares at a spot in front of him until it becomes two spots, the reaction occurs as a result of eye muscle fatigue. However, the subject or the hypnotist incorrectly *links* the seeing double to the hypnotic suggestion to do so. The same sort of linking can be done with sexual responses. I suspect, from engravings showing Mesmer's technique and from reports of his contemporaries, that there was a strong element of sexuality in his approach (as Franklin and the rest of the investigating committee made mention). Mesmer sat very close to his predominantly female subjects, with his legs on either side of theirs, and utilized what has come to be called "Mesmeric passes"—light strokes on arms, legs, backs, etc. As he did so, he spoke of animal magnetism passing from him to them. The tingling which many subjects report in this circumstance is usually linked by them to the power of the hypnotist to induce bodily changes in them.

Erickson's arm levitation induction method, in which the subject's arm floats "involuntarily" upward, can be analyzed in terms of similar linking maneuvers. This method begins by calling attention to the subject's hand. Does he feel the air around the hand that you have asked him to place firmly on his knee? Most subjects will immediately feel the cool air around their hands and, one hopes, will attribute the feeling to the hypnotist's command. If the hypnotist is lucky, the subject will have placed his hand flat on his knee, an uncomfortable position since the natural resting position of the hand is slightly cupped. With the hand pressed flat down, there will be a natural tendency for the palm to lift off the surface on which it is being held into the more natural and relaxed position. There will also be uncomfortable "restless feelings" in the fingers. The hypnotist begins by speaking of restless, spreading movement sensations that will cause the hand to feel buoyant and light. If he wishes, he can furnish an image that will enhance such feelings. For example, he can suggest a balloon underneath the hand. The initial movements of the arm will have occurred as a natural consequence of the situation, but the subject will have linked the movement to the hypnotist's commands. He will hopefully be unable to distinguish the exact line between what is physiological and what is volitional behavior. Thus, in arm levitation, while the restlessness experienced in the fingers and the palm rising off the surface are the result of the awkward position and fatigue (aided by the hypnotist's prediction), further levitation can be explained by generalization or by the subject's expectations and total involvement with the hypnosis.

Each linking maneuver should push the subject a little farther than is physiologically necessary. For example, when predicting to a subject who has extended his arm straight out in front of him that he will feel his arm as heavy and be unable to hold it up, one hopes that the arm will drop before it would necessarily do so on physiological grounds.

To tell a patient that he will be unable to keep his arm outstretched has frequently been labeled a "challenge suggestion." As another example, the subject might be asked to imagine his arm encased in lead or tied to an iron bar. The hypnotist then states, "*Try* and move your arm. *Try* as hard as you can for as long as you can." After ten seconds if the patient fails to meet the challenge, he is likely to be even more convinced that the hypnotist can hypnotize him. The emphasis on the word "try" implies that it is unlikely to be accomplished. When challenged, there is a small but distinct group of subjects, discussed in greater length in chapter 6 on reverse psychology, who experience a reversal of their will. That is, they become frightened and exactly what they fear takes place. Freud referred to this as counterwill or a perversion of will power.

Being "carried away" is the third and final stage of hypnosis. It has been called "the plunge" by Spiegel. Only a few subjects, perhaps 10 to 15 percent of those referred specifically for hypnosis, actually "take" the plunge. It is the stage in which the subject no longer doubts that the hypnotist can and does influence him and that he will exhibit all the phenomena that the hypnotist suggests. A generalization of linking takes place in a sense, a plunge takes place every time the subject goes beyond the physiological response of the linking maneuvers to one in which linking is no longer necessary. Most subjects who get this far into hypnosis assume a sleep model; they simply close their eyes and relax. Relaxation, itself, is responsible for patients not meeting certain challenges. However, those who take the plunge and allow the hypnotist to become what is sometimes called their "dream pilot" actually do not do anything that a highly motivated subject cannot do.

The sleep model is not always to the hypnotist's advantage. Subjects may remember what has occurred when the trance has ended and this recall may appear to them as a contradiction to their expectation of falling asleep. This can be dealt with by suggesting specifically to subjects that they will remember as much or as little as they wish to when they emerge from the trance.

Gill and Brenman (1959) have observed that occasionally the patient experiences an intense emotion such as crying during the induction. This rarely occurs after the induction phase. Also during the induction, subjects are likely to reveal secrets. For these two reasons, among others, it is not a good idea to hypnotize people at parties or just for fun.

As I have indicated, after the induction of hypnosis of any depth ("after involvement in the ceremony" is an alternative phraseology), a strategy is developed and utilized by the therapist. Many of these strategies can also be utilized without hypnosis. Frequently it appears to be a matter of taste and expectation on the parts of both therapist and patient whether or not hypnosis adds a useful dimension to the therapeutic experience. Hypnosis may facilitate the ability of some patients to concentrate, and some therapists may find it easier to issue commands and opinions in the hypnotic context.

Because many of the techniques used with hypnosis can be used without it, I shall review them as independent strategies in

the following chapters regardless of whether an induction procedure has been undertaken.

DIRECT SUGGESTIONS FOR IMPROVEMENT

There is always an implicit suggestion that the patient will
improve after a session of psychotherapy. Patients report
improvement following diagnostic procedures which have not
been explained as such to them. Occasionally it is helpful to
make such a suggestion directly. Some patients confuse their
greater hopefulness with an actual improvement, which gives
them a slight impetus to try harder at overcoming a problem.
This process can set in motion a snowballing improvement. Most
of the time, however, a more complicated procedure is required.

In hypnosis, direct suggestions can be made either during the
actual trance or posthypnotically. During the trance it is sometimes useful to make it clear that certain events can happen,
even if the patient doesn't think so. For example, if a man with a
paralyzed leg can make it move following the direct hypnotic
command to do so, the notion of eventual recovery in everyday
life is communicated. Hope is established. Even if his leg
remains paralyzed when he is out of the trance, the patient's recognition of the possibility of recovery is kept alive by this procedure.

The use of "posthypnotic suggestion" as a strategy for change
or cure dates back to the origins of clinical hypnosis. I began my
discussion of hypnosis with an example in which Rachmaninoff's
psychiatrist used this strategy. The most common suggestions
are that the patient will get better, that he is learning to cope
with his problems. Despite numerous reports that patients
respond well to posthypnotic suggestions, it seems in fact that
only those with high trance capacities can use them successfully.
Even then it is usually necessary to reinforce such suggestions in

subsequent hypnotic sessions, since their effects wear off rather quickly and seem particularly interfered with by sleep.

Freud (Breuer and Freud, 1895, pp. 100–101) reported an amusing episode in a case in which a woman came to see him concerning a problem with her gait: she could not walk unsupported, and used an umbrella as a cane. She was an excellent hypnotic subject, but Freud had no success using direct suggestion or by moving her legs during hypnosis. He finally became annoyed, lost his patience, and shouted at her, "This has gone on too long. Tomorrow morning that umbrella of yours will break in your hands and you'll have to walk without it, and from that time on you will never need an umbrella again!" Freud said later that he couldn't imagine how he could have been so foolish as to give a hypnotic suggestion to the umbrella! In fact, the next day the patient broke the umbrella under some pretext (she was beating time to a song with it). Freud reports that the patient had transformed a nonsensical strategy into a brilliantly successful one. Perhaps help like this from patients is more common than we recognize.

Mastering hypnosis frequently means developing an ability to induce a hypnotic trance or conduct a hypnotic ceremony convincingly. One can ask the patient in a hypnotic state to do such things as make his arm stiff or, alternately, allow his arm to float in the air. However, such demonstrations are not directly related to the problem brought for treatment (unless the patient's arm was bothering him). It behooves the therapist to incorporate into the hypnotic ceremony an additional strategy. On occasion the direct suggestion for improvement is all that is required; many hypnotists use one or another variation of this strategy. To go beyond this approach requires knowledge of other techniques discussed in the following chapters. It is often a matter of personal preference whether techniques to be described in part 2, on the midgame, are used alone or with hypnosis.

Part Two

THE MIDGAME

Hope is a good breakfast, but it is a bad
supper.

Francis Bacon

CHAPTER 5

Relaxation Techniques

RELAXATION has recently received considerable attention in both professional and popular publications. The nonpharmacological production of this state is said to have multiple medical and psychiatric benefits (Denniston and McWilliams 1975), and a bewildering array of religious, secular, occult, and psychotherapeutic techniques have been proposed to induce it (Regush and Regush 1974). The wealth of information, highly publicized techniques, and, to some extent, mystifying theory about relaxation together create a complex task for the clinician who wishes to use effective techniques but who does not wish to align himself with any one cult or fringe movement or to employ one technique exclusively and monotonously for all conditions.

Discussion of relaxation within a clinical framework poses several difficulties. Some problems stem from the profusion of techniques and their exploitation by commercial interests. Other problems originate because, as I have already discussed, mere belief in the possibility of obtaining relief from tension may be exceedingly important in bringing it about. It is thus difficult to determine which techniques, if conscientiously learned and applied, will induce relaxation, and which are equally effective "ceremonies" that will boost the patient's morale or in some other way operate in an indirect or "placebo" fashion. Furthermore, there are serious problems with the definition of such words as "tension," "relaxation," and even terms with generally acceptable textbook definitions, such as "anxiety" (Lewis 1967).

Although much of the area to be covered has been discussed by others in mentalistic terms which purport to describe states of increased creativity, of infinity, of immortality, an evangelic sense of mission, union with God, an altered or higher state of consciousness, being covered by a cloud of forgetting, experiencing a higher form of perception, visiting the soul's deeper regions, experiencing harmonious movements of pure thought, drawing near to God, communing with nature, spirits, other lives, and so on, this chapter attempts to categorize and integrate various nonpharmacological methods for obtaining relaxation from what is essentially a behaviorist position. It is assumed that all behavior is evoked by stimuli of either external or internal origin. Consequently, the behavior associated with or, in some views, synonymous with tension is assumed to be the response to certain stimuli. There are, then, two main approaches to relaxation. The stimulus can be modified, leading to reduction of the tension response and presumably a sense of relaxation, or one can seek to influence the response rather than the stimulus. Care must be taken in determining whether stimuli or responses are being modified. When terms like "meditation" are used, certain new skills are implied as the essence of relaxation. However, as we shall see, many meditation techniques simply block stimuli. Biofeedback, on the other hand, does not modify stimuli but in most cases seeks instead to modify behavioral responses.

The commercial exploitation of certain relaxation techniques is now a very visible aspect of our society, because big business, marketing, and publicity techniques have been widely used. Media coverage has been extensive enough for a fairly high proportion of patients in medical and psychiatric practice to have been made curious about the use of relaxation as an alternative to more traditional methods. A classification such as that proposed here can help in answering questions and in integrating some of the techniques into more traditional practice in a rational fashion.

TECHNIQUES DEALING WITH STIMULI

For the benefit of exposition, stimuli will be divided into covert and overt categories. In the simplest case a stimulus that provokes tension is overt and visible. That is, the stimulus responsible for a particular reaction could be identified as such by an observer, even though he himself might respond differently or not at all to the stimulus. Another class of stimuli is covert in nature. In these cases the stimuli are not easily recognized by an observer, although the subject, in most cases, can report that he was "thinking" or "picturing" something that made him tense. In some cases an observer might notice associated behavior, such as the subject mumbling to himself or having rapid eye movements suggestive of scanning a visual image (Rabkin 1963). The number of people one can notice mumbling to themselves when they think they are unobserved is surprisingly high, as are those who report so-called "daydreaming" about their problems (Singer 1974).

TECHNIQUES DEALING WITH OVERT STIMULI

Participation by the therapist. In contrast to the traditional role of interpretation, the clinician can try to alter the overt situation of the patient. For example, he can actively and consciously adopt an "advocate" role. In other situations he may act as an arbitrator or go-between, and attempt to reduce stress on a patient in that fashion. In a survey of requests made by patients as they entered a psychiatric clinic, Lazare and colleagues (1975) found that a fairly high proportion of patients seek such help.

While direct and intentional environmental modification has been increasingly adopted as a method of reducing individual or social tensions, there are also times when a therapist's restriction of his interest to the purely personal aspects of a patient's life can have inadvertent or unintentional effects on those around him. For example, the patient, unknown to the therapist, can reap certain advantages from "being in analysis." He can find that it enhances his social standing. Significant others in the patient's life, such as the patient's parents, can take the fact that their child requires psychotherapy to mean that they have been doing something wrong. They become more supportive, allow the patient greater privileges, and so on, changes which neither the patient nor the therapist sought to bring about.

Avoidance. One way to deal with stimuli that produce unwanted responses is simply to avoid them. Although among psychotherapists there is often an unreasonable prejudice against this solution, it is a rather common means of coping with stress. It can be achieved very subtly—as when a scientist remains in a location where there is very little competition rather than accept a job in a major research center. While avoidance can become maladaptive, as in phobias, there are occasions when the advice to avoid stimuli can be helpful. For example, in situations of loss, part of the recovery process is the gradual removal of stimuli that provoke mourning. I have already discussed the mother who left untouched for several years the room in which her deceased son had lived. His eyeglasses were on the desk. Predictably, she was still distressed. In another case a divorced wife found that she was unwilling to stop the stream of gossip about her ex-husband and that his apparent successful and carefree life was a constant source of distress to her. Her own mother, to be helpful, called three times a day to talk about the situation. In such a case avoidance can be a helpful "relaxation" strategy.

Reframing. From a transactional point of view it is common to distinguish between the stimulus per se and the context in which it lies—its frame. One way to reduce the reaction to a stimulus proper is to modify the context. The contribution of Ellis (1962) has been to develop the technique in which an unchanged stimulus or situation is "reframed" to appear different and less stressful. The glass is said to be half full rather than half empty. This method depends upon the notions of Epictetus, a crippled Roman former slave who is famous for his remark that "it is not the things themselves that disturb us but our opinions of them." The most common such reframing in psychotherapy is to convince a patient that a disastrous event was really a "learning experience." As another illustration, a depressed patient was severely distressed by the fact that his mother did not react with sympathy on hearing that he was contemplating suicide. The therapist's response was to be pleased with the mother's reaction, or lack of it, because it did not reinforce talking about suicide. The patient, seeing the lack of sympathy in a different light, became less distressed about his mother's indifference. Ellis, in using this technique, is careful to monitor the adjectives associated with the description of an event—words such as "horrible," "disastrous," and "awful" are avoided. The patient is cautioned to describe the event rationally and in neutral terms, asking himself what is the worst that could possibly happen. As a result, the frame of reference is likely to be more benign and what lies within it more acceptable.

Distraction. Any technique that successfully shifts the subject's attention from one external stimulus to another which is less anxiety provoking will relax the subject. Such techniques can include shifting the focus from a problem of the present to the supposed source in the early years of development, or conversely shifting the focus from a stimulus in the near future (an examination in the next two weeks) to an immediate sensation in the consulting room. In the latter technique the subject is asked where is the anxiety, pain, or depression in his body, what "color" it is, whether it is diffuse or can hold water, and so on. Such bodily preoccupation shifts the subject's attention away from the source to an exceedingly abstract and imaginative expression of the reaction. Hypnotic pain relief frequently operates by distraction in similar ways (Hilgard and Hilgard 1975). The stream of unrelated images can distract the patient from the pain or prevent the addition of a mental anguish component to the total pain experience.

Techniques that use a distraction strategy, like many others, do so with the addition of various ceremonies and explanations which have been discussed in part 1. Taking the technique out of context frequently appears to make it seem ridiculous. For example, in a recent review of new techniques (Harper 1975) Gestalt therapy is illustrated by a description of a therapist asking the patient, "What is your foot now doing?" This general effort to shift the patient's attention from the source of his difficulty to the response or to totally irrelevant bodily sensations appears less effective than it actually is in the total context of psychotherapy, supported by impressive and popular intellectual theories and equally impressive ceremonies.

Exposure. Research with phobias and compulsions has suggested that prolonged exposure to the overt stimulus (a bridge in a bridge phobia, dirt in a handwashing compulsion) leads in a relatively short period of time (an average of eleven sessions in one series) to an extinction of the fear, avoidance, or rituals (Marks 1976). There are many techniques that have as their ultimate effect the exposure of the subject to the feared object. The exposure can be in fantasy or in reality, under high or low anxiety conditions. Low anxiety, fantasied exposure called "desensitization in fantasy," is often accomplished by using an independent relaxation technique such as hypnosis or progressive relaxation training (see below) and then presenting the patient with a hierarchy of increasingly fearful images. "Implosion" and "flooding" are the terms used for exposure under high anxiety conditions in fantasy and in vivo, respectively. Other techniques depend upon praise or some other reward as the patient approaches the feared object ("operant conditioning"). Blocking a ritual or compulsion (for example, handwashing) as a technique seems to be effective because it leads to exposure (for example, to dirt).

"Reciprocal inhibition" is one of the notions used to support low anxiety fantasied or in vivo exposure. The basic concept is that when one pairs a stimulus or condition that is relaxing (for example, food, sex, or assertive behavior) with the fearful stimulus (a bridge in a bridge phobia), there are two competing responses. If the fearful stimulus can be attenuated by placing it at an imagined or real distance or in some other way reducing its intensity, then the strong incompatible response will "counter-condition" the subject. The originally fearful stimulus will begin to be linked with the pleasant response. The uniqueness of this method has been criticized in light of the fact that exposure is still the underlying process.

Many other treatments which at first appear somewhat sophisticated seem to have exposure as their basis. For example, in a case in which Spiegel (1960) (see chapter 7) substituted a lion and bear phobia for a severe dog and cat phobia, what immediately followed the hypnotically induced or aided "symptom substitution" was exposure to dogs and cats. The patient's parents, in fact, bought a dog soon afterward.

Learned tension and learned relaxation. Although at first it appears contradictory, it is possible that a patient has been rewarded by those around him when he appears tense. When he has a worried look, when he dwells upon tension-producing subjects, he may receive sympathy and even material rewards. In such a circumstance it would be expected that the tension would increase. For example, a young woman obtained a job about which she was somewhat apprehensive. She found that when she called her father, who lived 3,000 miles away and from whom she rarely heard, she could reestablish a supportive relationship with him. She called him nightly. He responded with unaccustomed warmth and concern, and she grew more and more tense. When this process was interrupted, she felt considerably better.

By the same token, a relaxed and confident attitude, particularly in times of stress, can also be rewarded by those around and by what subsequently occurs. Those fortunate to have learned this response are quite successful coping with stresses. It has been suggested (Marks 1976) that "stress management" might be routinely taught in school. Knowledge of a wide range of methods, as suggested in this chapter, might be useful as a point of departure.

TECHNIQUES DEALING WITH COVERT STIMULI

Many behaviorists are content to deal exclusively with overt stimuli on the assumption that, whatever covert process occurs, there is ultimately an overt one that can be better handled. For example, in the case of a bridge phobia there is the overt stimulus of the bridge and the covert stimulus of the train of thought which conjures up the line of cars falling into the water far below. It is the former stimulus that would be dealt with. There is, however, an extensive literature on covert stimuli.

Blocking. Perhaps the oldest and most popular relaxation techniques are those that simply block the covert stimulus, the source of the tension. Thus if someone is troubled by an imagined dialogue, its interruption by the method of repeating an irrelevant word will relax him. Prayer has also been advocated for this purpose. Many members of modern cults (e.g., Hare Krishna) seem to be mumbling "blocking words" to themselves when they are seen on the streets. Their adherence to the cult evidently depends in part upon the absence of independent thought, which is obstructed by this mumbling ritual. When the covert stimuli are visual in nature, if the patient is imaging tension-producing stimuli, then a blocking visualization might be appropriate to relieve the tension. For example, a tense subject might be encouraged to imagine himself on the beach and his problems on an outdoor movie screen far away on the horizon. Counting sheep is both a blocking visualization and verbalization which is ineffective today because its comic reputation does not accurately portray the demanding and totally consuming process of actually counting several thousand sheep as they run from one field to another through a small opening in a fence (not jumping over it). There is probably spillover from a verbal (auditory) technique to visual stimuli, and vice versa. Music, prayer, chanting, concentrating on the movement of one's breath through the nasal passages, repeating a one-word "mantra" (as in Transcendental Meditation), attending to the visual images one sees when the eyeballs are pressed or to the sound that one hears with one's hands over one's ears, or attempting to taste the "living waters" by rolling one's tongue so far back as to taste nasal mucus (the last three techniques are advocated by Guru Mahara Ji's Divine Light Mission), going to the track or to horror movies, or watching television, are all blocking techniques.

Certain blocking techniques are maladaptive. In some cases eating binges lead to such guilt in the overweight individual that it takes the patient's mind off other subjects that are more anxiety provoking (for example, spinsterhood), and hence eating becomes a rewarding blocking maneuver. Certain patients learn to scare themselves with thoughts of cancer, their parents dying, and so on, because such ideas actually block more real and immediate concerns that would be much more disturbing.

Electric convulsive therapy has been used as a disruptive technique (Rubin 1975). The procedure is to ask the patient to think about those covert stimuli or themes that trouble him; as he is so doing, ECT is applied. The treatment is said to function by disrupting the patient's ability to continue to concentrate on the unpleasant theme by creating a retrograde amnesia.

Marijuana smoking also seems to function at times as a disruption. Many users of marijuana find it difficult to think about relevant concerns when they are high. The ringing of the telephone and horns in the street have about the same relevance. Thinking about an important problem or examining the patterns made by the ashes in an ashtray can have the same degree of significance to a person who is "stoned."

Stopping. "Thought stopping" is similar to a blocking technique, but it depends on the patient's ability to pick up a different train of thought following his recognition of covert anxiety-provoking stimuli. The patient either voluntarily stops the distressing train of thought or is taught to do so by the therapist, who takes advantage of a startle response. When the patient signals that he is well into the train of thought that is anxiety provoking, the therapist startles him by yelling "Stop" (Wolpe 1973, p. 211–213). Another technique consists of training the patient to snap a rubberband which he wears on his wrist whenever the target train of thought is identified.

TECHNIQUES DEALING WITH RESPONSES

As in our discussion of stimuli, responses will be divided into overt and covert, using the same criterion of that which is readily observable. For example, overt shy, unassertive behavior can be easily observed, while chronic hyperventilation is usually not noticeable to any but the most astute observer.

TECHNIQUES DEALING WITH OVERT RESPONSES

Educational programs. There are now numerous programs which seem to fall halfway between psychotherapy and education, such as assertiveness training, marriage encounters, occupational guidance, and family therapy or Parent Effectiveness Training (P.E.T.). Many publishers now issue self-help books and colleges give a wide range of extension courses on subjects such as drugs, widowhood, and modern sexual roles. With the increase in skills and effectiveness of responses, maladaptive tension responses are presumably reduced. It has been suggested that such programs reduce the possibility of symptom substitution by providing adaptive alternatives for patients.

Associated fantasy. Assertive, effective, optimistic people are frequently the way they are because of their fantasies or expectations about the future of their endeavors. Conversely, most unassertive behavior is accompanied by a fantasy which would make such behavior reasonable. A young man will not call up a new young woman for a date if his fantasy is one of a humiliating rejection. Certain individuals seem to have learned how to develop goal-directed fantasy. This was most strikingly shown by the already-quoted work of Spanos (1971), who gave hypnotic subjects the apparently impossible task of forgetting the number four. Those who were successful seemed to have a visual image that assisted them. In another study (Hilgard and Hilgard 1975) in which a young woman was asked to anesthetize her arm, she imagined herself the Venus de Milo! Dreams of glory and Walter Mitty fantasies are quite common in those who are effective in coping with the environment. The reverse sort of fantasies abound in those who fail to be effective. For example, a young man was in a bus that was being driven recklessly. He thought that he should speak up but then imagined the driver turning around, drawing a pistol, and shooting him.

Taking this associated fantasy into account, it is possible to suggest or "implant" positive or negative thoughts, depending upon whether one desires to support or discourage certain behavior. There is considerable literature related to the implantation of positive thoughts. Prayer, for example, is sometimes employed in this fashion. In the occult techniques popular today, "treating" or "treating for" some positive event consists merely of repeating several times a day that some good event is going to happen. In a method that appears to be transitional between the occult and psychotherapy, Ray (1976) has published a guide to the use of "affirmations" in which she requires that patients who seek her help with sexual problems, write, record, or say to themselves ten to twenty times a day a set of phrases such as "I am more and more pleasing to myself every day. I am beginning to like myself as a man. I no longer have to hate myself to please my mother. I am more and more lovable." This bears considerable resemblance to the original work of Coué and self-hypnosis techniques which require the patient to put himself in a trance and then recite to himself an affirmation ten times a day. Spiegel (1970) uses this method for such problems as smoking, obesity, and phobias. There have been more technical efforts to introduce such positive thoughts, for example, in depression, utilizing the so-called "Premack Principle" (Homme 1965) of linking one behavior (reading a list of positive attributes) with a high-frequency behavior (e.g., smoking).

Cautela (1967) has developed the technique of implanting aversive thoughts to be associated with a habit problem (overeating, alcoholism). He first induces a relaxed and possibly more receptive state in his patients (see below) and then suggests that they imagine they are about to perform the undesirable behavior, following which he describes the subject's becoming nauseated in the most vivid terms. Presumably they link the unwanted behavior with the nausea (see Appendix D).

TECHNIQUES DEALING WITH COVERT RESPONSES

There is a group of techniques that seeks to create relaxation by changing the bodily response. In this case an alternative response occurs but it is not viewed as tension by the subject. For example, a small but definite group of people overbreathe when exposed to certain stimuli. They develop hyperventilation symptoms of dizziness, palpitations, paresthesias, carpal-pedal spasms, and an assortment of other traits. They often feel as if they are having heart attacks, appear in emergency wards, and are misdiagnosed as "anxiety attacks." Such a patient can be treated by suggesting that he carry with him at all times a brown paper bag into which he breathes when the attack first begins. This procedure apparently keeps the level of carbon dioxide high enough in his lungs to prevent symptoms from developing. Other suggestions include schooling oneself to breathe through the nose at times of stress (i.e., keep one's mouth closed). If these procedures are successful, the only change that is being made is in the response. (Many Eastern meditation techniques concentrate on breathing. Some are designed to serve as distractions and others actually to create a mild form of hyperventilation whose dizziness suggests an altered state of consciousness.)

One of the most common forms of covert tension responses appears to be muscular in nature. In some cases this is localized to the neck or forehead; in others it is a more generalized increase in muscle tone. Jacobson (1938) developed a relaxation technique that depends upon a pendulumlike swing from extremely tense muscles to flaccid ones. The modern version of this technique, progressive relaxation training, divides muscles into groups and encourages the subject alternatively to tense and relax them. Eventually the groups are combined, and ultimately relaxation of the muscles is linked to repetition of the word "relax." It is perhaps the same mechanism that is responsible for relaxation after strenuous exercise. Activities such as yogic exercises, Chinese exercises called tai chi chuan, jogging, and swimming all seem to function as a means of relaxing those who respond muscularly. Massages apparently also assist and, in addition, help in the identification of those whose muscles are tense. If a subject does not respond positively to massage, it is unlikely that his muscles are tense.

Investigators working with technically assisted knowledge of results or "biofeedback" have predominantly concentrated on response modification. One of the most widely used forms of biofeedback consists of training someone to relax his muscles assisted by the use of electrical voltage readings from a target muscle group, usually the frontalis (forehead). Galvanic skin response has also been used for biofeedback, but it appears to have been abandoned for more sophisticated devices. Any bodily response that can be brought to awareness—even in an unsophisticated manner—could potentially be used to train a subject in its modification. For example, whenever one swallows one ingests a small portion of air. If, as the result of certain stimuli, one swallows more frequently—perhaps because one salivates more—there is increased air in the stomach. The result can be gas pains, eructation, or flatus as a symptom of tension. If one can modify swallowing behavior, most of which goes on out of awareness, there is a possibility that the symptoms can be eliminated. In this case a tight collar would qualify as a biofeedback device in much the same fashion that a scale functions as biofeedback in weight control. Biofeedback, however, has an appeal that goes beyond its technical assistance. Some observers feel that it epitomizes American pop culture, being simultaneously highly sophisticated electronically and antiintellectual.

Biofeedback using brain wave patterns is difficult to classify. Alpha waves, for example, characterize an absence of visual images. If that is the case, training to maintain a state of alpha waves would block visual images that might be producing tension responses. Such a technique would therefore be classified as a stimulus-blocking method. Theta waves, on the other hand, are said to be associated with creative moods, fantasy, and daydreaming. These are presumably pleasant fantasies and might serve to block other stimuli. In any event, these brain wave patterns are associated with relaxed states and are reported to be effective in training certain subjects to relax.

VIEWPOINTS ON RELAXATION TRAINING

THE CASE AGAINST RELAXATION

One of the observations made by clinicians attempting to utilize progressive relaxation training is that certain subjects appear frightened of the relaxed state. It has been the general procedure to reassure them that it is their unfamiliarity with relaxation that makes them frightened, and that there is actually nothing to fear. It is implied that familiarity with the state of relaxation will result in adjustment. In a sense, what is implied is that exposure will lead to comfort. This appears to be true, but it must be remembered that exposure will also lead to comfort with realistically dangerous experiences, for example in combat or with factory machines. In addition to the patient's own initial sense of vulnerability, there are several converging lines of experimental evidence to suggest that deep relaxation might have untoward effects. Relaxation techniques appear similar to those methods that have been developed for inducing a "hypnagogic state." There is a reduction in the level and variety of sensory and proprioceptive input, a shifting to a state of passive volition, and the maintenance of a state of arousal sufficient to permit awareness and fend off sleep (Schacter 1976). Under these circumstances a new idea can be received with less critical appraisal; a fearful thought can have greater impact and influence. Sensory deprivation studies have also suggested that under these circumstances the subject is more receptive. Earlier studies suggested that subjects become massively disorganized and gravely impaired in their functioning with prolonged sensory deprivation. More recent studies suggest that with less extensive and less strict sensory deprivation, subjects become more suggestible but not uncomfortable (Smith 1976).

It is interesting to note that both Freud (Breuer and Freud, 1895) and Moebius in the last century attributed hysterical symptoms to a "hypnoid state," which is similar to the conditions described above. Moebius writes:

The necessary condition for the (pathogenic) operation of ideas is, on the one hand, an innate—that is, hysterical—disposition and, on the other, a special frame of mind. We can only form an imprecise idea of this frame of mind. It must resemble a state of hypnosis; it must correspond to some kind of vacancy of consciousness in which a merging idea meets with no resistance from any other—in which, so to speak, the field is clear for the first comer. We know that a state of this kind can be brought about not only by hypnotism but by emotional shock (fright, anger, etc.) and by exhausting factors (sleeplessness, hunger, and so on) (quoted in Breuer and Freud 1895, p. 215).

While relaxation techniques appear to be the antithesis of brain-washing, it is possible that for certain more susceptible individuals a state of deep relaxation is, in fact, a state of vulnerability to influence similar to that reportedly induced by stress. This can be employed for the benefit of the subject and might be effective in new treatment methods (particularly habit control), but subjects are justified in being concerned. Of course, subjects who habitually prefer to control events will resist efforts to induce relaxation. However, relaxation appears to be a vulnerable state about which it is reasonable to be cautious.

From a different critical vantage point it has been pointed out that relaxation as such is not the goal in life. A certain amount of stress is useful. Total relaxation does not facilitate growth, learning, discovery, or even great pleasure; mild tension is far more effective in accomplishing such ends. It is primarily relaxation defined as the absence of incapacitating anxiety that is a positive end-state, and it is in this sense that it constitutes a therapeutic goal. Total relaxation may also be the total absence of reinforcement, which then subjects the individual to the possibility of depression. Self-centered pursuit of sybaritic luxury in the guise of the medical necessity for relaxation has been criticized as the "new narcissism." This can apply to the subject who retreats from life and joins a meditation center or the subject who shirks responsibility to jog two hours a day "for his health."

Finally, one of the tried-and-true methods of relaxing in the face of anxiety has been the "counterconditioning" support of loved ones. Their ministrations evoke reactions that are incompatible with tension and are reciprocally inhibiting to anxiety. It is important to consider what naturally occurring "relaxation techniques" are available before introducing artificial ones. Wolpe (1973), for instance, points out that the sexual drive in a young adult male with impotence can be counted on to be more powerful than anxiety. With only slight modification of circumstances, the problem often can be overcome by using what is inherent in the situation rather than by introducing additional techniques. Wolpe's suggestion is to interdict intercourse and extend foreplay. I wish to emphasize that the availability of highly publicized but artificial relaxation procedures should not lead to their use prior to a careful search for intrinsic possibilities that can achieve comparable results.

THE AUTONOMIC NERVOUS SYSTEM AND THE HYPOTHALAMUS

In my presentation I have taken the position that relaxation is the absence of certain stimuli and of certain responses. Benson and his colleagues (1974) believe that there is an integrated hypothalamic response which results in relaxation. They quote favorably the work of Hess (1957), which attributes this response to a zone located in a specific area of the anterior hypothalamus. The response is said to be mediated by the parasympathetic nervous system following electrical stimulation of this zone. Hess is of the opinion that this response is the naturally occurring balance to the response which Cannon labeled the "fight or flight" reaction. It is seen as a protective mechanism against stress. Benson's approach is to adopt Hess' work and think in terms of relaxation as a response, that is, the presence of something superimposed on whatever is impinging on the organism at that time.

There is both a difference in emphasis and a difference of opinion between the neurophysiological work and that being presented here. The difference in emphasis stems from whether the patient is approached from the inside out or the outside in. It seems reasonable to suppose that whenever an organism is described as tense or relaxed, his body responds in some fashion consistent with that state. Work with the hypnagogic state suggests that in the relaxed condition there is a shift from dominance of the sympathetic to the parasympathetic nervous system and a "resetting of the hypothalamic balance" (Stoyva 1973).

The difference of opinion stems from whether the response can be stimulated from within, so to speak, or whether it is in reaction to the stimuli impinging on the organism. Benson's review of blocking devices, his acknowledgment that distracting thoughts should be passively disregarded, and that a quiet environment is conducive to "provoking" the "response," all suggest to me that, if there is such a center and such a response, it is currently controlled in practice predominantly by modifying input into the nervous system. We may work more like the canine than we like to admit: a dog falls asleep when he is not attending to some stimulus. Observations that might be construed to support the notion of a self-activating center concern the effects of excitement, stress, exhaustion, and so on—"brainwashing" when deliberately created. The assumption here is that a balancing or restorative function is activated by the organism when stress becomes too great. The techniques of flooding or implosion in which a subject is exposed in vivo and in fantasy, respectively, to the full impact of that which disturbs him could be construed to succeed because they stimulate the relaxation response. However, alternative explanations have been offered in terms of learning stress management with any of the techniques discussed above. At present, the concept of an integrated relaxation response does not lead to any therapeutic technique not arrived at by the stimulus-response framework.

CHAPTER 6

Reverse Psychology

A RECENT clinical report (Hare-Mustin 1975) describes a four-year-old child, Tommy, who was brought for treatment because of daily temper tantrums. Instead of trying to stop the tantrums, the therapist advised that Tommy continue them. After considerable family discussion, it was decided that the safest place for him to do so would be in the upstairs hallway. During the following week Tommy had only one tantrum, and on that occasion he was taken to the tantrum place. Another family discussion then occurred during which it was agreed that there would be a tantrum time as well as a tantrum place. By the third week there were no tantrums at all. The therapist expressed concern that perhaps the rate of change had been too rapid and suggested in an offhand way that Tommy might want to have a tantrum the following week—of course at the appointed time and place. A follow-up after nine months confirmed that no further tantrums occurred.

Many techniques that seem to resemble this case are commonly regarded by the general public as varieties of reverse or negative psychology, because the objectionable symptom is encouraged rather than attacked. In the professional literature such techniques can be grouped in three major categories. Some are behavioral in origin, such as negative practice, conditioned inhibition, and satiation. Other techniques are psychodynamic in derivation, such as paradoxical intention. A third group consists of techniques that are more cognitive in nature, usually considered part of the "double bind" literature.

Several important theoretical issues are raised by these often neglected techniques and observations. Hypnosis can be defined in their terms, the pathogenesis of certain symptoms can be better understood, and the double bind hypothesis and the notion of symptoms as power tactics can be reevaluated.

BEHAVIORAL TECHNIQUES

NEGATIVE PRACTICE

In 1928 Knight Dunlap proposed the revolutionary principle that patients who wished to rid themselves of certain problems, notably tics and habits, could do so by the active, conscious technique of "practicing" them. Dunlap called the method "negative practice." The psychologist Wakeham (1928) then attempted to use this method to deal with habitual errors he made when playing certain selections from Bach's Toccata and Fugue in D minor on the piano. He practiced the selections daily for two weeks with the wrong notes deliberately inserted. On the fifteenth day he played the pieces without error several times. He then went on to apply the theory and technique of negative practice to typing errors. He found a subject who consistently repeated the beginning letter of a word at the end of a word, e.g., "wordw" for "word." After one day of negative practice, errors of this type dropped from 52 percent to 12 percent of the total errors.

Dunlap (1928) himself reported that he had success with his method with tics, typing errors, stammering or stuttering, thumbsucking (in four- and five-year-old children), enuresis, masturbation, and homosexuality. If one stops to think what the climate must have been like in the 1930s, when he advised a bedwetter, masturbator, or homosexual to "practice" his symptom, one can get a feeling for the impact of this technique at the time. Clearly, his definition of a habit was rather broad, but his method, which he never described in detail, evidently influenced a variety of behavioral conditions.

A more recent paper by Lehner (1954) attempts to correct Dunlap's omission of detail by giving specific instructions, including a suggested verbatim introduction to be delivered to the patient (Appendix E). It should be pointed out that Dunlap's lack of specificity about his method was the result of his belief that the method itself was not the crucial element in symptom removal, but rather that patients were impressed, startled, and had their hopes built up by his instructions for negative practice.

CONDITIONED INHIBITION

The techniques suggested by Dunlap were adopted by learning theorists, who offered a different explanation for their effectiveness. They believed that the recommendations for negative practice were effective because they led to the development of "conditioned inhibition" (Kendrick 1960).

Conditioned inhibition is explained as follows: When one repeats an act over and over again in rapid succession, called "massed practice," fatigue sets in. For example, if I were required to lift a twenty-five-pound weight quickly many times, at a certain point my muscles would become tired. If I were encouraged to continue, I would begin to ache; eventually, no matter how hard I tried, I would be unable to lift the weight. A somewhat similar situation occurs with a habit or tic. If I repeat the tic in exactly the same manner as fast as I can for a long period of time, a "fatigue" sets in, but this time the "fatigue" is presumably not in the muscles. This more central fatigue is called "reactive inhibition." As it builds up, it forces me to "rest" or not perform the tic.

The reactive inhibition or fatigue has many of the same

unpleasant characteristics of an unfulfilled drive such as hunger. Whatever one does to reduce it is reinforced by the dissipation of the reactive inhibition, just as what one does to reduce a hunger drive (press a button for food) can be thought of as being reinforced or rewarded by the dissipation of the hunger. In a similar fashion, the rest from lifting a twenty-five-pound weight is very pleasant. It is more than just "not lifting the weight." It is a special rewarded event.

When I am forced to rest by reactive inhibition, this interruption—this "not performing the tic"—is rewarded by the unpleasant reactive inhibition becoming dissipated. As a result, what was once a forced rest becomes a "habit of not performing the tic," a negative habit, or "conditioned inhibition." At some point this negative habit of not performing the tic will become stronger and stronger and overwhelm the original tic.

The original habit or tic, the problem itself, does not improve with practice past a certain point. It is known that the strength of such habits increases up to a point and then reaches a maximum, an asymptote. Thus, further performance of the tic or habit cannot increase its strength beyond a given point. This being the case, with massed practice the habit of not doing the tic increases in strength until it equals the strength of the habit itself, canceling the problem out.

Continuing my analogy to lifting weights, if I lifted weights in massed practice until dreadful fatigue developed and the rest period that followed became much more desirable than the lifting of the weights, I would eventually stop lifting the weights altogether. I might even begin to avoid them. What might happen to me might resemble the experience of the college president who once quipped, "Whenever I feel like exercising, I go inside and take a nap." While this remark was interpreted to be merely a witticism intended perhaps as a slur on athletic activities, it may have represented conditioned inhibition resulting from an experience in gym classes that resembled massed practice.

SATIATION

Another explanation offered by learning theorists for the effectiveness of the techniques we have been discussing is that of satiation. Having a child write a dirty word on the blockboard 500 times transforms what was originally a titillating act into a boring punishment. Repeating over and over again something that originally led to reinforcement often seems to satiate the subject.

Ayllon (1965) used what he called the procedure of "stimulus satiation" with a female mental patient who had a nine-year history of towel collecting and storing. About twice a week the nurses used to remove towels from the patient's room. In his experiment the nurses were instructed to stop removing towels and, in fact, to give the patient towels throughout the day without comment. The number of towels given her per day was increased from seven the first week to an average of sixty per day by the third week.

Ayllon reports, "during the first weeks of satiation, the patient was observed patting her cheeks with a few towels, apparently enjoying them." By the fourth and fifth weeks the patient exhibited comments such as "Get these dirty towels out of here!" After the total towels in her room reached 625, the patient began to remove them herself. This continued until she had almost no towels and maintained for the next twelve months the rate of one or two towels per week in her room.

RESPONSE BLOCKING AS A STRATEGY

Whereas negative practice and conditioned inhibition are techniques for the removal of particular symptoms, response blocking has been advanced as the more general underlying strategy. It is assumed that the symptom is being maintained by its apparent success. For example, in the old joke a gentleman tears papers and throws them out of the window of the train on the way to work in order to keep the lions from attacking the train. When his traveling companion remarks that there are no lions in this vicinity, the subject remarks, "See how successful the paper tearing is!" The apparent success of his action reinforces it by what is called "negative reinforcement," the absence of lions. Response blocking functions by preventing the symptom—the paper tearing—until the patient "realizes" that his dreaded outcome will not occur. It is a technique that forces exposure to the fearful stimulus. Thus, if the subject could be forced to stop tearing paper by negative practice, conditioned inhibition, or simply by taking his paper away from him, he would experience intense anxiety for a period of time and then it would gradually stop as none of the dreaded outcomes, none of the lions, appeared.

For most of us the environment functions to block symptoms. For example, compulsive handwashing requires proximity to bathrooms and the good fortune to have a job that does not get one's hands dirty. A garbageman cannot develop that symptom as easily as others because he would lose his job. Even if there were a disposition in that direction, his response would be blocked. Although most of us have environments that are inhospitable to symptoms, there are a few unfortunate individuals who do not. For example, it is said that a well-known reclusive multimillionaire suffered from a series of compulsions. He was constantly trying to avoid dirt, did not shake hands, opened doors with paper towels, and so on. Needless to say, those with vast power and wealth experience few external blocks of any kind. He died of the complications of malnutrition directly attributable to his compulsions. I came across another example of wealth potentiating symptoms in my clinical practice. In the course of treating a family, I visited their house. After a while I realized that there was something odd about it: there were no doors. Even in the bathroom there was a clever arrangement of mirrors so that there appeared to be no doors. The shower curtain was transparent. It turned out that the mother was afraid of closed places, but she had the money and the power to indulge herself. For most of us that response is blocked by the reality of our lives. However, great wealth is not the major cause of compulsive symptoms. I use it here only because it offers a very clear example. In many cases parents seem to indulge their children by not blocking responses. Either there is a split between mother and father, so that there is effectively a blank check for the child, or there is overt indulgence.

When I was a resident at Bellevue Hospital in New York City, I had the opportunity to interview many denizens of the Bowery, the nearby skid row. For reasons I no longer remember, I asked many of the men how they could live the life that they did. Weren't they scared? Some of them took the time to explain to me that I was suffering from a misconception. I thought their lives were dreadful and dominated by such perils as freezing in the winter and starvation. They told me that at some point they had realized that none of these outcomes would occur. This "psychopathic insight" was behind some of their activities. I realized that I was somewhat like the man tearing newspapers. I was working hard, studying, and "achieving" because I was trying to keep the lions away from my door. What they had realized was that there were no lions. There are some people who develop a similar psychopathic insight about such behaviors as extramarital affairs, lying, going through red lights, or overt criminal activities.

Most psychotherapies attempt to make the patient less anxious. Thus a patient with a compulsion might be given a relaxation strategy (hypnosis, progressive relaxation training, biofeedback). This is sometimes successful. However, when the symptom seems to be maintained by negative reinforcement—by its apparent success at warding off a dreaded outcome—blocking the symptom has been reported to be more successful. Compulsions in particular seem to respond to blocking. However, it is sometimes very difficult to block effectively a compulsion such as handwashing by using an overt strategy, particularly when it is backed by intense anxiety. A patient might be hospitalized and kept away from the sink. In general, therapists who have attempted this approach find it difficult and trying, and usually do not keep doing it because it is too hard on them. In such circumstances, negative practice and conditioned inhibition appear as attractive strategic alternatives that achieve the same goal.

PSYCHODYNAMIC TECHNIQUES

COUNTERWILL

Before he became absorbed in the observations and theories that led to the formulation of psychoanalysis, Freud and his colleagues observed that certain subjects, who were regarded as constitutionally inferior, reacted to worries in a peculiar manner which eventually led to the occurrence of the very event they were so concerned about avoiding. For example, when carrying a tray of delicate glassware, the worry, "I might drop these," could occur to anyone. However, these presumably abnormal people worried so much about it that they ended by dropping the tray. It was thought that the idea of dropping the tray, called by Freud a *distressing antithetic idea*, is split off from consciousness, develops its own power, and acts as a counterwill, taking over the subject's body and causing him to enact the distressing idea in spite of his conscious will to prevent it. In his explanation Freud personified willpower, an explanatory concept employing mental faculties which will be examined critically below.

In many of Freud's cases the origins of symptoms were not readily attainable from his patients. In time he became increasingly absorbed in problems of recall and disorders of memory, which eventually culminated in his psychoanalytic formulations. However, in his early work he did address himself to the curious dilemmas of patients, suffering from what he called *counterwill*, who tried too hard to prevent something from happening and worried excessively about it.

Freud reported several interesting cases in which the counterwill prevailed. For example, in the case of Frau Emmy Von N. (Breuer and Freud, 1895), her symptom was a ticlike noise that she could not prevent herself from making. This arose when the patient was taking care of her child, who had been very ill during the day, convulsing, but had fallen asleep toward evening. The exhausted mother—disposed, perhaps, by the exhaustion*—thought to herself, "Now you must be absolutely quiet, so as not to wake her." The clicking noise first appeared at this moment, but passed after a brief period. However, some years later the patient was driving through the forest when a violent thunderstorm began and a tree beside the road just ahead of her coach was struck by lightning. The coachman had to rein in the horses suddenly and the patient thought to herself, "Now, whatever you do, you must not scream, or the horses will bolt." At this moment the ticlike clicking noise came on again and persisted until Freud saw her.

Although Freud's cases involve serious pathological consequences of counterwill, instances of it are almost daily occurrences in most peoples' lives. Some common examples include attempting not to blush (and blushing more), trying not to giggle in church or to cough when someone is asleep, trying to diet or avoid forbidden fruit of all sorts, trying to prevent incontinence, to urinate in a doctor's office or a public restroom, or to fall asleep. Other examples of everyday counterwill are stage fright, trying to concentrate on school work and not fall asleep at one's studies, attempting to hurry, and being calm in a graveyard.

INDUCED COUNTERWILL

When Freud developed the notion of counterwill, the patient seemed to do to himself whatever was necessary to create the

* See discussion on vulnerability of relaxed subjects in chapter 5.

pathology. It was assumed that the phenomenon did not occur normally and that the patient must have some predisposition— Frau Emma's exhausted and frightened state or some more lasting constitutional problem predisposed her to the episode of counterwill. However, for purposes of illustration let us suppose, contrary to Freud's report of the case, that a well-meaning physician said to Frau Emma that her child must sleep and that she must make absolutely no noises at such times. This "injunction" to remain silent might be the moving force in creating excessive anxiety and excessive intention (effort of will). In this case the process that created the pathology is now, at least in part, a transaction between two people.

The "challenge" in hypnotic induction is an effort on the part of the hypnotist to foster the development of hysterical counterwill. When he says, "No matter how hard you try (suggesting that the patient try excessively), you will find that you are unable to raise your arm," he is hoping the patient will experience counterwill. He will try to raise his arm and find it impossible. In discussions of hypnosis it is always necessary to remind the reader that "not being able to raise an arm" can occur for other reasons as well (the patient can report that he was "so relaxed" that he did not try—this is not what is meant by counterwill).

It is also possible to observe similar instances of induced counterwill between parent and child. For example, if a child is afraid of a dog, it seems only natural for a parent to say, "You have nothing to be afraid of. Don't worry. You'll be all right." In most cases this appears to do no harm. However, there are times when such urging creates counterwill. The child tries to be relaxed in the presence of a dog and worries that he will panic. This sort of approach to anxiety can increase it or, in the case of a fear of dogs, create a dog phobia. Spiegel (1974) reports on a dog phobia patient with whom he was working successfully with a combined self-hypnosis and reciprocal inhibition strategy. The patient was a grown woman who, pleased with her success, told her father about her progress when he came to visit her. She went next door and got a dog to show her father what she had been doing. As the dog approached her, her father began, "Don't worry. There is nothing to worry about," and her phobia returned. She had not mentioned to Spiegel that this had been the well-meaning strategy of her parents in response to her fear of dogs.

It is interesting to note that Spiegel's usual approach to a dog phobia is to first state that it is perfectly reasonable to be frightened of wild animals. I might add that statistics suggest that if you are a child it is perfectly reasonable to be frightened of dogs, particularly unfamiliar ones. This sort of remark might be more therapeutic than had been previously supposed if the origin of dog phobias is frequently the result of being told that there is no reason to worry about them.

Other areas about which patients may be inappropriately reassured are painful experiences or procedures, and achievement anxiety in school. Perhaps the most important area is in therapy itself. Once some success has been achieved in solving a problem (a dog phobia, for example), there is the possibility of counterwill occurring about the successful treatment, with the therapist urging the patient to continue to improve. Such an atmosphere can worry the patient about a relapse as he tries to hurry his cure along. When this is suspected, Watzlawick and colleagues (1974) have suggested, it is necessary to "prescribe a relapse" or, at least, ask the patient to "go slowly." The case involving tantrums that begins this chapter includes an illustration of this technique.

THE TREATMENT OF COUNTERWILL BY COUNTERWILL

In the therapy of spontaneously occurring counterwill, one of the most obvious treatment strategies is to relieve the anxiety. This could be accomplished by a relaxation strategy from whatever source is possible. For example, simple reassurance of the impotent patient that he will regain his potency is often sufficient. There is, however, another strategy that seems designed for these problems, which Frankl (1960) called *paradoxical intention.*

In essence, paradoxical intention operates by inducing a process that is the opposite of the counterwill that is occurring. If I am worrying about fainting and my intention to attempt not to faint is causing me to become more faint, then, if I try to faint, the same mechanism, whatever it is, will operate in reverse by preventing me from fainting. This has been called in the hypnotic literature *Baudouin's law of reversed effort* (1920). It has also been called "experiencing the experience" and "getting into your feelings." In the latter terminology, a patient who is trying to avoid loneliness, for example, might be encouraged to experience it or "to get into his feelings." When he tries to do this, he finds that he is not lonely any more. This phraseology is often met in psychodynamic psychiatry. In pain relief it has been found helpful to ask, "What color is the pain?"

One of Frankl's cases illustrates the treatment process:

A young physician came to our clinic because of a severe hidrophobia. He had for a long time been troubled by disturbances of the autonomic nervous system. One day he happened to meet his chief on the street and, as the young man extended his hand in greeting, he noticed that he was perspiring more than usually. The next time he was in a similar situation he expected to perspire again and this anticipatory anxiety precipitated excessive sweating. It was a vicious circle; hyperhidrosis provoked hidrophobia and hidrophobia, in turn, produced hyperhidrosis. We advised our patient, in the event that his anticipatory anxiety should recur, to resolve deliberately to show the people whom he confronted at the time how much he could really sweat. A week later he returned to report that whenever he met anyone who triggered his anticipatory anxiety, he said to himself, "I only sweated out a liter before, but now I'm going to pour out at least 10 liters!" What was the result of this paradoxical resolution? After suffering from his phobia for four years, he was quickly able, after only one session, to free himself of it for good by this new procedure (Frankl 1960, p. 522).

Frankl has accumulated many illustrations of this technique, including a case in which hallucinations were treated successfully. Jackson (1963) published an experience with a paranoid man who thought that his office was bugged. Jackson became appropriately concerned and insisted that he and the patient explore every nook and cranny of the office to find the microphone. As the search proceeded, the patient became more and more unsure and somewhat embarrassed about the whole notion, but Jackson would not let the matter rest until they had done a thorough job. Following this experience, the patient plunged meaningfully into a description of his relationship with his wife, about whom he had good reasons to be suspicious. Jackson suggested this technique for the treatment of paranoid delusions. He called it *prescribing the symptom,* and later used it with other symptoms, including enuresis.

Newton (1968) has tried to explore what the exact criteria might be for using this technique, which he calls *symptom scheduling* to avoid any theoretical alignments. He divides the variables into three groups:

Symptom variables. The symptom must be expandable. Ever-present anxiety would be a poor symptom, while handwashing a certain number of times a day would be excellent, since it lends itself to increasing the frequency. Current acute problems are better than low-grade chronic ones. Interpersonal problems are better than individual ones. Problems that are stressful are better than those that are only mildly inconvenient.

Schedule variables. The schedule should be expandable, interpersonal, stressful. The schedule should stress the patient even more than the symptom. It is necessary to offer the patient a rationale. In many cases just the simple "we have to do something crazy to get rid of something crazy" will do. Humor is helpful. "Try to have the best case in recorded history." (Frankl, too, emphasizes humor, which I suspect has some hidden significance that might warrant future study.) One

should be as specific as possible about the symptom to be scheduled. There should be time for the patient to discuss the strategy
at the end of the session, exercises in the session for reluctant
patients, and a follow-up appointment soon after the patient
begins in order to make sure that he is following the schedule
and understands the instructions. Sometimes an introduction to
another patient who has used the technique successfully is
helpful.

Therapist variables.   The therapist must be comfortable with
a directive orientation, have a degree of patience, and believe
that such a technique may work.

COGNITIVE TECHNIQUES

SYMPTOMS AS TACTICS

Haley (1963) discusses the situation in which a wife
"requires" that her husband be home every night because she
has anxiety attacks when she is left alone. Haley feels that the
wife is controlling the situation while denying that she is doing
so. For Haley, when we attempt to control a relationship while
denying it, we are exhibiting symptomatic behavior. There are
unquestionably subjects who fit his description and who use
symptoms for interpersonal power. However, in this case it is
possible that the wife wants very much to let her husband leave
the house. She dreads the idea that she might become anxious
and tries as hard as possible to remain calm. The result of this
strong effort and her excessive anxiety creates a perversion of
will, the phenomenon of counterwill already described. Her husband's responsibility in the onset of her symptoms is limited to
that which he does to make her try so hard or worry excessively,
if he does anything at all. He may need to go to work, he may
threaten her with divorce if she isn't normal, or he may do absolutely nothing but act in such a loving and accepting fashion that

she desires to be a loving and considerate wife to him and let him have freedom of movement. Under this revised set of possible circumstances, which admittedly Haley does not report, the wife's symptoms are not the result of an effort to control but an instance of counterwill.

A case I saw that is somewhat similar to Haley's anxious wife involved a thirty-year-old married housewife who developed a bad cough. It's origins are unclear; she may have developed an allergy, she may have had a postnasal drip from overuse of nose drops to which she was addicted, or there may have been little or no underlying organic problem. The patient was pregnant and had had sufficient difficulty with her husband in the past for him to have left her for a short period of time. The cough became particularly severe when her husband returned from work. By the time they went to bed she was coughing constantly, keeping her husband awake. She began to worry that he would leave again just because of the cough. She went to several specialists, each of whom managed to worry her further. One spoke about the effect of coughing on her pregnancy, another about the drastic measures that would have to be taken to cure her of the cough.

The patient thought that her cough might be "psychiatric" because she noticed that it became worse when her husband came home. She thought she might be punishing him for having left her or that she really hated him underneath. However, on the surface it was clear that she wanted very much to please him and that, when she realized that he was about to come home, she would try to control the cough; it was then that it would become particularly bad.

I suggested that the patient try to cough when her husband came home, that she try as hard as she could to have a particularly bad spell of coughing (paradoxical intention). The patient thought it strange but followed the instructions and the cough disappeared.

Haley's analysis of hypnosis suffers from the same criticism:

his examples could just as easily be illustrations of counterwill. For example, Haley (1963) refers to a report of Erickson's in which the latter was asked to demonstrate hypnosis on a subject who apparently volunteered the information that he could not be hypnotized. (Such subjects are often mentioned in the literature on hypnosis.) Erickson brought the subject to the lecture platform and said, "I want you to stay awake, wider and wider awake, wider and wider awake." The subject promptly went into a trance. Haley sees the situation as a struggle for control in which Erickson used certain tactics. The other possibility is that Erickson, sensing that the subject was already trying hard to remain unhypnotized, increased the subject's effort of will and his anxiety until he was able to get a perversion of will, or counterwill.

For Haley, when a patient closes his eyes under hypnosis, he is denying that he did that particular act deliberately. The closing of the eyes is like a symptom in Haley's model because it is denied as a responsible act. However, it *can* be an instance of counterwill. A patient might close his eyes for any number of reasons: because he is relaxed, because he desires to be cooperative, because (as Haley emphasizes) he complies while denying that he is doing so. These hardly seem to qualify for the term "hypnosis," although in therapy it might be helpful to allow the term such a broad definition. An instance of counterwill, however, does seem to both therapist and patient to be a special event worthy of being labeled.

Finally, Haley's analysis of paradoxical intention suggests that by getting the patient to repeat his symptoms, the therapist is gaining control over them by making them occur at his direction. "The basic rule of brief psychotherapy would seem to be to encourage the symptom in such a way that the patient cannot continue to utilize it" (Haley 1963, p. 55). Here he assumes that the patient has a use for his symptom, that it is an interpersonal tactic, and that the therapist outwits the patient in a kind of psycho-jujitsu. The patient in some cases can be shown to have a use for his symptom, but there are other times in which this is not the situation, as in my illustrations of counterwill.

There does not seem to be any rule of thumb by which one can distinguish between a symptom that is a tactic and a habit that is being actively reinforced by some ongoing process. Sometimes there are instances of symptom substitution suggesting an underlying utility for the symptom. However, in most cases the therapist must judge for himself. If the patient seems genuinely fearful of the consequences of his symptom and is focused intently on its removal, perhaps counterwill is in operation.

SYMPTOMS FROM PARADOXES AND DOUBLE BINDS

In the 1950s a school of psychiatry led by Bateson took a great interest in transactions within the family. Attention was directed to messages or communications that were likely to create pathology. I have already indicated that induced counterwill might result from certain injunctions. Although there was no reference to counterwill, Bateson and his colleagues began to study instances of similar communication (Bateson et al. 1956; Watzlawick, Beavin, and Jackson 1967). They became intrigued by a category of counterwill problems that they classified as the "Be Spontaneous Paradox." The category includes such injunctions as "I want you to dominate me," "You should enjoy playing with the children like other fathers," and "Don't be so obedient." It seems to me that by worrying and trying too hard to enjoy children, to dominate, or to be spontaneous or independent (to use the examples just cited), counterwill can develop. However, the emphasis in Bateson's work was on the formal, logical, and potentially problematic qualities of such injunctions. Because they seemed paradoxical, they were thought to confuse those who received them in some mind-boggling way that produced severe cognitive pathology characteristic of schizophrenia. A wide range of statements were thought to constitute a new category of communication called a *double bind*. The term is admittedly rather vague and has as yet escaped adequate definition (Rabkin 1976).

I have tried out several paradoxes on individuals without making them anxious. None of my listeners seemed to react to the apparent illogical nature of my requests. For example, one rather withdrawn and borderline woman, when asked to "be spontaneous," smiled, tapped me on the shoulder, and said, "There." She did not seem disconcerted by the paradox. I had not worried her about her ability to be spontaneous or induced her to try excessively. She was quite pleased with her reaction. On the other hand, such an injunction can make things worse. In a tense marital situation the wife, who earns more than her husband, feels that she has the upper hand, that her husband is not "man enough," and that he can't make decisions that she can make with ease. When she explains this to him and asks him to be more dominant, her request exacerbates their difficulties.

Finally, a careful reading of the literature reveals that in many cases patients do not actually communicate in paradoxes, but that the investigator reduces what has been said to a paradox. The wife in the above example does not come out and say, "I want you to dominate me." She tried hard to describe a desired relationship. She cares a great deal about her husband, but is unhappy and perplexed.

The literature of the double bind also refers to double binding the double bind, or a "therapeutic double bind" placed by the therapist on the patient, with the result that the symptom is removed. Examples are not easy to find, but the terminology sounds similar to using counterwill to cure counterwill.

Since it is not clear what is referred to as a double bind, one cannot be sure that it does not include something above and beyond counterwill, but it does seem that many of the illustrations could be examples of counterwill. It is furthermore conceivable that counterwill could be responsible for certain pathological thought patterns. All one would have to do is be worried about whether one could think logically and then try excessively to do so. The result could be incoherence. Whether this is actually the origin of certain thought disorders is entirely speculative. However, if Jackson can cure paranoia and Frankl can terminate hallucinations with paradoxical intention, it is likely that *in these specific cases* something like counterwill was in operation.

STIMULUS MANAGEMENT AS AN ALTERNATIVE
TO THE CONCEPT OF COUNTERWILL

A description of the phenomenon of counterwill identifies a condition that is both common and the source of considerable psychopathology, yet it does not offer us an adequate explanation. We can no longer be satisfied with a theory (and a terminology) that depends on the outmoded concept of mental faculties. That is, to imply that there is a faculty of the mind called "willpower" and that under certain circumstances this faculty splits and forms two opposing wills (one of them being the counterwill to which I have been referring) is now found wanting by most mental health professionals.

An alternative to the concept of counterwill can be found in the notion of stimulus management. Our cognitive apparatus appears designed to select certain stimuli over others. For example, we generally attend to the spoken voice and filter out extraneous noise such as street sounds. This is impressed on us when we listen to a tape-recorded conversation because the mechanical device does not perform this filtering service. Some of our ability to attend selectively may be inherent in feature detectors within the receptor organs, but a portion is acquired. For example, one of the lessons a child must learn after he has mastered riding a bicycle is to look where he wants to go rather than at that which he wants to avoid. If he is riding a bicycle on the sidewalk and seeks to avoid pedestrians, he must correct his natural tendency to look intently in their direction with the result that he rides right into them—an apparent example of counterwill.

Most of the time we have no difficulty in attending selectively to the appropriate features of the settings we are in. However, errors can occur. Most of them are inconsequential, but occasionally they produce undesired and pathological responses. For example, in order to prepare successfully for an examination, a student must focus on the academic material presented in the course. If he is worried about failure he may begin to think about his professor's critical remarks, his parents' distress, the end of his academic career, and other fantasies that impede his efforts to study. Certainly, with such thoughts (covert stimuli) in mind, his ability to study would be impaired, and this might be interpreted as an instance of counterwill. In this example impairment of the selective process leads to the interference of an activity: studying. In other instances such impairment may lead to initiation of a new (unwanted) activity as a result of failure to keep certain stimuli under control.

Treatment that exhorts the patient to undertake the feared behavior is successful because ultimately it removes the preoccupation—particularly if there is a ridiculous or humorous quality to the request. Such requests remove the fear and the morbid fascination and ultimately the stimulus. While in most cases it is adaptive to keep one's eyes on what one fears, so to speak, the instances of which we are speaking suggest that it is also important to be able to block stimuli. The mythical prototype is of the snake that dances in such a way as to fascinate its prey, who is transfixed by the snake's weaving and bobbing and slowly moves toward it. While there is no actual evidence that this occurs with snakes and their prey, the solution for such prey would be to take their eyes off the snake and think about the goal of finding a lair that is impregnable. Such a train of thought and incoming stimuli would lead to different responses and safety.

Examined in the above light, counterwill appears to be a failure of stimulus management. Reverse psychology need not be the only treatment. The actual goal is the seeking of appropriate stimuli. To suggest that a child riding a bicycle try to hit pedestrians might achieve the same results as teaching him to look at where he desires to go because he would cease to be fearfully fascinated by his potential target and, on his own, shift his attention to a safer path. Thought stopping and thought blocking might also change the stimulus picture.

Several years ago I treated a young professional who was in a fairly high place in public life. His complaint, that of homosexuality, was distressing to him, against his deeply felt religious beliefs, dangerous in view of his public position, and had proved resistant to both psychoanalytic treatment and religious advice. Once or twice a week he would be overcome with the desire for a homosexual contact. At these times he would wander through parks or men's bathrooms, so-called "tea rooms," and finally make some sort of contact with a willing partner. Afterward he would be overwhelmed with disgust and remorse. On occasion he would vomit upon contemplating what he had done. This pattern had gone on for many years.

My prescription to him was that on Monday, Wednesday, and Friday he would go to a local Turkish bath which was a meeting place for homosexuals, and there have five homosexual contacts to orgasm, whether he wanted to or not. Several other rules were put in effect to protect this major strategy. The patient soon found that he was failing to have five homosexual contacts but was having massages instead. He found that he had become much less interested in the whole subject. We cut down the visits when they became a considerable burden to him, eventually terminating them altogether. He married soon after and, on last seeing him, about five years following his treatment, he had no further symptoms in this area. The entire episode was as if it had happened to a different person. He was amazed and encouraged me to publish the case.

This case seems to resemble each of the techniques we have

discussed. Dunlap (1928) reported using negative practice with homosexuals, and presumably this case would be an illustration of his method. At the same time, conditioned inhibition might be offered as an explanation, since the patient began to prefer massages rather than homosexual contacts. He might have developed a habit of not having homosexual contacts. Satiation might also be advanced as an explanation of the cure. The prescription that I recommended to him could be called symptom scheduling, paradoxical intention, prescribing the symptom, getting into one's feelings, and placing the patient in a therapeutic double bind. Furthermore, by suggesting to the patient that he must follow what I told him to do and then proceeding to recommend that he continue to do what he had been doing all along, I obtained a relationship with him in which I was the dominant figure. The only way for him to reassert his independence was to stop his symptomatic behavior. In placing the patient in such a position Haley might say I was outmanipulating him. By scheduling his homosexual contacts I may have removed the ever-present thought (stimulus) which would eventually lead to the abhorrent response. The injunctions "Don't put marbles in your nose" or "Try not to think of a pink elephant," although phrased in the negative, still can present a vivid stimulus. Removal of the thought "don't have homosexual contacts" would be an instance of stimulus management.

Further research must determine which technique is appropriate under what circumstances. We must also determine the extent of difference among techniques, and whether alternate treatment strategies concentrating on stimulus management might add to our understanding of these problems and treatment methods.

CHAPTER 7

Symptom Substitution,

Transfer, and Sharing

HISTORICALLY, one of the cautionary predictions of psychoanalysis has concerned the likelihood of symptom substitution in cases where the therapist was imprudent enough to treat only the symptom rather than the presumed underlying cause. For years, concern about symptom substitution was a major deterrent to strategic attempts to deal directly with symptoms. Only recently has it been recognized and demonstrated that this is not the invariable or even typical consequence of symptom cure. While the myth of the inevitability of symptom substitution is currently seen for what it is, and there is now widespread license for treatments that concern themselves with symptom removal, there is a danger of the pendulum swinging too far. Symptom substitution does occur, and it is profitable to inquire under what circumstances this happens. Furthermore, while symptom substitution is by no means inevitable, as once claimed, this is in part due to a relatively unnoticed phenomenon—the transfer of symptoms from one person to another. In this chapter I shall discuss the problem of symptom substitution briefly as a means of introducing the related problems of symtom transfer, transformation, and sharing. In so doing, light is shed on some possible therapeutic strategies for symptomatic treatment that might profitably be explored.

SYMPTOM SUBSTITUTION
AS PROBLEM AND SOLUTION

PROBLEMS OF SYMPTOM SUBSTITUTION

The task of proving or disproving the validity of the notion of symptom substitution has been complex. Initially it was not a scientifically studied phenomenon, but rather a clinical observation passed along from one therapist to another. Over time, attitudes became polarized, with some investigators doubting whether the phenomenon existed at all and others believing that it was the inevitable outcome of symptom removal. At present, most investigators seem to agree that symptom substitution does occur, although they differ in regard to the conditions under which it is likely to do so. They further agree, in general, that it is a relatively infrequent outcome of symptomatic therapy and therefore should not be seen as a deterrent to such treatment.

Among the relatively few therapists who had experience in dealing with the treatment of symptoms, those who used hypnosis were able to provide some information regarding the probability of symptom substitution following symptom removal. With habit patterns, pain syndromes, and neurotic symptoms such as airplane phobias, hypnotists were fairly successful in removing symptoms without new ones cropping up. In fact, they frequently observed what they termed the "ripple effect" (Spiegel and Linn 1969), in which removal of a symptom in one area was followed by "spontaneous" improvement in other areas. The ripple effect is actually the converse of symptom substitution.

In some cases hypnotists did observe symptom substitution. These cases seemed to share common patterns. One such pattern was observed to consist of virtually miraculous symptom removal by hypnosis. The patient perceived this as humiliating, and consequently such cure was followed by the appearance of another symptom, often worse than the one it replaced. Particularly with hysterical symptoms such as a paralysis, instant hypnotic cure embarrassed the patient. It is one thing to take a long, painful journey to Lourdes and perform numerous religious ceremonies in the company of others in like situations and *then* to experience a miraculous cure, but it is quite another to have a hypnotist conjure away a long-standing habit or symptom with no preparation. To deal with this problem, hypnotists did not assume that the symptom and its substitute had some joint underlying causal relationship that led to the substitution. Instead, they concerned themselves with the task of preserving the patient's dignity. They learned to avoid "wonder sessions" and miracle cures and gave patients time and preparation, for example, by suggesting that the symptom would gradually disappear over a period of time such as a week or two.

A second situation associated with symptom substitution concerned unsolicited symptom cures in which the patient's secondary gains detracted from his motivation for cure. In such cases the patient is typically pressed into therapy by well-meaning relatives. If and when some therapeutic maneuver removes the symptom, it is often replaced by another, just as effective and often considerably cruder.

For example, an elderly woman was forced by her husband and her sister to see a psychiatrist. The chief complaint was that of headaches so incapacitating that she could do no housework or cooking. "Fortunately" her husband was retired and took over the household chores. The psychiatrist suggested that when she had the headache she could stay in a hotel or at home, providing that she did not eat anything. With this coercion the headache went away, but she developed a mystifying "oppressive weight" on her shoulders that completely incapacitated her and essentially achieved the same results.

From a behavioristic point of view, symptom substitution has been explained by the patient's having a hierarchy of maladaptive responses. With the removal of the most prominent, the second comes into play. It has also been suggested that if a patient does not learn the relevant coping skills in dealing with a problem, removal of a symptom is likely to be followed by some other maladaptive behavior.

Furthermore, the exact definition of "symptom" and how it differs from "problem" or just unhappiness has never been too clear. Other methodological issues include when and how long to look for a substitution, and whether certain conditions (e.g., ulcers) are more likely to be followed by a substitution than others (e.g., enuresis) (Montgomery and Crowder 1972).

SYMPTOM SUBSTITUTION AS A STRATEGY

Although the general approach in psychotherapy is to attempt to remove a symptom altogether, there are times when a substitution, or a change in symptoms from one that is disabling to one that is not, can be helpful. Rather than being something to be feared, symptom substitution can be used strategically. Rather than an unwanted side effect, symptom substitution can be a therapeutic goal.

Spiegel (1960) reports a case of a teenage girl who all her life was afraid of dogs and cats. When she was little this was considered cute and amusing, but by the time she was seen in therapy it severely limited her social life, which in turn depressed her and caused her school achievement to decline. It was the school difficulty that prompted her parents to bring her for treatment. During a hypnotic session Spiegel discussed with her the fact that it is normal for people to be afraid of animals, *wild* animals. Partially as the result of hypnotic suggestion and partially of the ingenuity of the girl herself, Spiegel was soon notified that the patient had dropped the cat and dog phobia and had told her father that she did not want to be brought near the local zoo (itself a highly unlikely event). She had substituted a fear of lions and bears for cats and dogs. This case has been followed for some time. The patient eventually dropped the fear of the zoo animals, did well in school, and did not have a recurrence of the phobia. She is married and has children of her own.

Psychoanalysis itself may be seen as a symptom substitution process. The psychoanalyst who deemphasizes current problems (for example, the self-starvation in anorexia nervosa) and manages to shift the focus to the underlying personality structure, as Bruch (1975) apparently is capable of doing, is in fact substituting one concern for another. A transference neurosis is acknowledged as a substitution. This approach or emphasis must be distinguished from the giving of insights or interpreting as a therapeutic method.

Interestingly, the same sort of shift of focus from ongoing problems can be achieved by emphasizing the so-called "here-and-now" in terms of immediate physical sensations and feelings. Gestalt therapy frequently makes this shift from problems to raw bodily sensations.

SYMPTOM TRANSFER:
PSYCHOLOGICAL STUNT MEN

SYMPTOM TRANSFER AS A PROBLEM

Wangh (1962) reports a case in which a six-year-old frightened her younger sister by telling her scary tales when their parents were out for the evening: "When the younger one becomes upset, the older one assumes the role of protector; she pets and reassures the little sister. These bare facts easily invite the interpretation that the older sister herself had been anxious, that she had gotten rid of her anxiety by arousing this emotion in her younger sister" (Wangh 1962, p. 456).

What is startling about symptom transfer is that it opens up an entirely new field of clinical study. Psychodynamic theory had hitherto concentrated on the patient's "imaginary" problems. For instance, in the above case a psychodynamic theorist would expect the older child to "project" her fear on an appro-

priate "object" (i.e., her mental representation of some person),
not actually to create a frightened alter ego.

According to psychodynamic theory, symptom transfer was
originally regarded as a rare and rather pathological mechanism.
An initial step toward the understanding of symptom transfer
was the theoretical recognition that a person vicariously participates through an unconscious identification with another person
who, on his own, was gratifying certain needs that the first
person also had. Alter egos and extensions of ego feelings
beyond the actual self have also been noticed. Anna Freud
(1946) referred to the alter ego as a "proxy," and Sperling
(1944) labeled the other in these situations the "appersonand."
Benedeck (1937) describes the use of an analyst as a superego.
Stein (1956) suggests similar phenomena in marriage, and
Heiman (1956) in the bond between a man and his dog. But in
all these cases the proxy, alter ego, or appersonand was just a
handy figure with whom an imaginary relationship could exist.
The other was not himself affected by the entirely personal and
private dynamics which were taking place. For instance, a movie
star is not personally affected by adoration from a distant fan.

A breakthrough occurred in the psychoanalytic literature
when Eissler (1949) suggested that society might actually influence some of its members to act out their forbidden wishes.
Later Johnson and Szurek (1952) described how parents might
subtly encourage delinquent behavior on the part of their child,
and thereby benefit by vicariously living through the forbidden
delinquency and also expressing hostile impulses toward the
child, whom they could then punish severely. Such a parent
might listen to his child tell of delinquent acts with frank wonder
and pleasure on his face, a response which does not go unnoticed by the child, but then the parent might punish the child
when he is done recounting his adventures. These various observations represented a breakthrough because they reached
beyond the "imaginary" framework to actual transactions.

Activities of interest to the psychoanalyst took place in the inner world of the patient's mind. Rarely there might be a spill-over, as in the Johnson and Szurek study, but this was assumed to be the result of the powerful arousal of id impulses and limited to basic unconscious drives. These observations remained as curiosities. Wangh reported several fascinating cases concerning "the evocation of a proxy"—someone to stand in with another's problems, a psychological stunt man, *created* by the patient:

> Mrs. T. . . . had come for analysis because of a severe agoraphobia. Her past history included one period of depression and two episodes of mania, for which she had been hospitalized. When her sixteen-year-old son began to stay out late at night, she would wait for him for a while. Then she would wake her husband, a severe hypochondriac, from his barbituate-induced slumber. She easily aroused his anxiety to the point that he would storm out of the house, pace up and down the sidewalk for hours, engulfed alternately by waves of rage and anxiety, until the boy came home. In the meantime, Mrs. T. herself retired to sound sleep, from which she was awakened only when her snarling husband and truculent son staggered into the bedroom. Then she would get up and chat with the boy about his evening's adventures over a late night snack (Wangh 1962, p. 459).

Wangh mentions several other examples. Iago in the play *Othello* is overwhelmed with jealousy which he needs to discharge. He does so by arousing the same emotion in Othello. Wangh mentions that among homosexuals it is a kind of game to stimulate the jealousy of the partner. On closer examination Wangh has discovered that they themselves suffer from jealousy in their family. They avoid this feeling by making someone else jealous, by transferring the jealousy.

SYMPTOM TRANSFER AS A STRATEGY

As in Spiegel's case of therapeutically induced symptom substitution, symptom transfer can be a therapeutic maneuver. I was called to a general hospital to see a girl in her twenties who had been hospitalized several times with schizophreniclike symptoms. She was on a surgical ward awaiting a thyroidectomy. She had begun to show signs of decompensation and the surgeon was understandably concerned. In speaking with the patient it became clear that the patient's mother had periodically "given up worrying" about her, and it was at these times that she had had to be hospitalized. The treatment in this case was to worry the hospital staff. By adopting the attitude that the surgical nursing staff would be happy to know that a psychiatrist was waiting to be called, such as by suggesting that his name and telephone number be taped to the front of the patient's hospital chart and that the recovery room staff be informed that he was standing by ready for action, I induced the staff to begin worrying about the patient. The patient, seeing the concern for her well-being everywhere, sailed through the operation without incident.

In a similar case an exceedingly unstable young woman with a history of suicidal gestures became pregnant. Her psychiatrist became anxious and telephoned her obstetrician, who also became infected with the anxiety. The two doctors kept in constant touch about the condition of the patient, who, knowing of their anxious concern, delivered a healthy baby without incident. The problem ultimately became the anxiety of the doctors, who were as anxious after the delivery as before. The author, who knew the psychiatrist socially at the time, suggested that he ceremoniously do whatever people did in his family when someone had a baby. He gave the patient a baby present and found that his anxiety left him at once.

SYMPTOM TRANSFER
IN OPEN AND CLOSED SYSTEMS

OPEN SYSTEMS: EVIL

If suffering or a symptom can be transferred once, the victim might transfer it a second time, and the next victim a third time.

If there are no barriers to its transfer, if we are dealing with an open system, it might be transferred forever. This thought preoccupied Simone Weil, a modern French religious philosopher, who believed that evil could be defined as just such a chain (Tomlin 1954). She believed that evil spreads and flourishes in the world as it is passed on from victim to victim in the form of suffering. In this manner a single evil act, e.g., transfer of symptoms, may pass from person to person in an endless chain in which each experiences relief after causing another to suffer in his place.

I once had the unfortunate experience of looking out the window of a hospital just as a young girl jumped off the roof of the building across the street. Wandering out into the hospital corridor exceedingly distressed by what I had just witnessed, I met a casual friend to whom I described in detail the horrible scene, complete with sound effects. My victim's or "proxy's" face and demeanor fell in a mixture of the very horror and revulsion I had experienced, while I had a sudden and dramatic sense of relief, exactly as if I had shifted a heavy weight from my shoulders to that of my colleague's. He staggered off to pass the burden to still another person, while I, puzzled by my sense of relief, ate a hearty lunch.

CLOSED SYSTEMS: PSYCHOLOGICAL HOT POTATO

Weil (Tomlin 1954) did not take into account the possibility that the suffering about which she writes might not be discharged into the world in general, but is kept instead within a certain circle of people. In this case the symptom is bounced back and forth from one person to another in Ping-Pong or hot potato fashion, achieving nothing and, in fact, adding remorse to the original problem. Some of the earliest observations of symptom transfer were recorded by Jackson (1968), a pioneer in the family therapy movement. It was such observations that stimulated him to look at the family from a systems point of view.

A young woman undergoing psychotherapy for recurrent depression began to manifest increasing self-assurance. Her husband, who initially was eager that she become less of a burden to him, called the psychiatrist rather frequently and generally alluded to her "worsening" condition. The therapist had not made an appraisal of the husband; and when the extent of the husband's alarm became clear, he had become too antagonistic to enter therapy. He became more and more uneasy, finally calling the therapist one evening, fearful that his wife would commit suicide. The next morning he shot himself to death (Jackson 1968, p. 10).

Speck (1965) has written about the transfer of illness phenomena in families that he calls "schizophrenic." He believes that the transfer phenomena are practically daily events among members of these families with members who are schizophrenic:

We have repeatedly observed in hospitalized patients that one of the crucial phases in treatment is around the time of discharge from the hospital. Both schizophrenic patient and the family members feel increased tension. It is extremely common for the patient to have shown marked amelioration of psychotic symptoms in the hospital, but to have to be readmitted within a few days or weeks after return to his family. Nearly as common is the phenomenon of the primary patient's maintaining his improvement, but another family member living in the home is admitted to the hospital, often with a similar illness. I know of three cases in the last year where a family member suicided within the first month of a schizophrenic patient's discharge from the hospital as much improved . . . (Speck 1965, p. 225).

In these closed systems, whatever is set in motion reverberates back and forth among the elements of that system and cannot be discharged. In certain situations a pattern or cycle to those reverberations can be discerned. When a therapeutic intervention improves one member of the closed system, what is actually happening is simply that another member is being made to suffer. This seems to be one of the potential drawbacks of closed systems, particularly if they are close-knit. Taking this into account, Speck reports that he has treated nonsymptomatic members of a family with tranquilizers as he attempts to work with the "sick" member, in order to prevent transfers of symptoms from occurring.

SYMPTOM TRANSFER AND TRANSFORMATION

What sometimes happens in transfer phenomena is that an identical condition is replicated, as when a child frightens another about a fear she herself has, and then experiences relief. However, this is not always the case. Frequently there is not only a transfer but a substitution as well. In this case the combination can be called a *transformation*, as when a son improves from cognitive pathology (e.g., schizophrenia) and a father becomes depressed.

As an example of this phenomenon, I was once having a coffee break prior to a meeting when one of the participants entered the coffee room down in the dumps, hardly able to muster the strength to go to the conference. He appeared to be about to transfer his burden to me. I quickly stopped him, explaining what I had in mind. The other doctor then "changed the subject" and began to talk about his experiences in the Air Force, which were at first amusing but unaccountably began to resemble events in all bureaucracies, even those of the state hospital in which we found ourselves. Before long I found that I was feeling terrible, shaking my head about waste, corruption, and the hopelessness of it all. When it came time for the conference my colleague felt fine, and I was the one down in the dumps.

THE COMPETENCE DIMENSION

Symptom transfer itself can be examined from the point of view of competence. That is, some individuals seem to be more adept than others at transferring symptomatology. In this view, a really competent paranoid manages to have enemies, i.e., to be actually persecuted. If he is a virtuoso at being paranoid, those enemies get into trouble themselves, and a transfer of suffering is achieved.* It is only the chronic, pathetic, and incompetent paranoid who claims, for example, that there is a machine in the local high school that is emitting special rays influencing his precious bodily fluids. It is possible to see these symptoms as an effort to transfer certain burdens that have been passed on to him or acquired in some other fashion, *except* that in this case the maneuvers are done so badly that they achieve nothing except to make him appear strange in the eyes of others. It is at this point that such a person can be banished to a mental hospital and relief obtained from the entire Ping-Ponging system—until, of course, such a person is "cured" and attempts to reenter the community.

In considering symptoms such as paranoia, we can thus argue, contrary to the opinion of psychoanalysts, that the imaginary symptom is less competent, if not actually sicker, than the transferred symptom. Of course, in either case we are dealing with evil, competent and incompetent. Janet (1925) describes Irene, a case of hysteria, who is the victim of a competent paranoid friend's maneuver:

A young woman had lived for some time with a woman friend of whom she was extremely fond. One day she was stupefied when her friend accused her of making love to an elderly man. After some scenes between the two friends, Irene had to leave the house. She was able to exculpate herself fully from the charge, but she says, "I did not succeed in confounding my accuser, in humiliating her, in revenging myself upon her." For eighteen months after this incident, Irene remained ill, suffering from abulia, from invincible inertia, unable to sleep and equally unable to work, tormented from moment to moment by obsessions concerning the affair, by impulses to seek out the quondam friend, to make a scene in her house, to confound her, and although everyone was perfectly satisfied that *the whole trouble had arisen out of her friend's morbid jealousy,* she could not "liquidate the situation," and she was interminably

---

*See chapter 8 for a more detailed discussion of paranoia.

confronted by the same event without being able to get beyond it (italics mine) (Janet 1925, p. 955).

In a preliminary observation of three patients with obsessions, there were frequent interactions with others in which repetitive and senseless questioning by the patients occurred ("Do you think my face is too fat?" "Will I be fired from my job?" "Should I end the letter in X way or in Y way?") in the typically "sticky" fashion of obsessionals. Simple answers or reassurance only led to a repetition of the questions, even though they had been answered adequately just the minute before. The circumstances which terminate such a questioning bout appear to be when the person being questioned becomes upset and aggravated. At that point the patient has a moment of relief which seems to resemble a transfer phenomenon. This relief may be the reinforcement for the questioning. In most cases it is a relatively inefficient transfer technique which allows the patient only intermittent reinforcement. However, intermittent reinforcement schedules are known to be a powerful method of creating persistent behavior. In this view the transfer may constitute one of the bases of the symptom.

While obsessives seem to have some capacity to transfer their burdens, patients with panic states or phobias often seem to feel there is nobody who is sympathetic to their plight. When others begin to share their worries they improve somewhat.

RELIEF FROM SYMPTOM TRANSFER

In the case of open systems, Weil (Tomlin 1954) suggests that evil is continually accumulated and spreading. Such observations would be grim were there not mechanisms that work to obtain relief from suffering, whether the suffering is caused by other people, that is, transferred from them, or is the result of life circumstances (such as significant criticism, rebuff, or failure). These mechanisms are of particular interest to psychotherapists.

MARTYRS AND BANISHMENT

Since symptom transfer depends on the act of causing another person to suffer, if someone is not willing to transfer suffering, it must be ended at that point. Weil has considered this possibility and has suggested that a martyr can stop a chain of evil by taking the burden on himself. Her life was lived in such a fashion. A tuberculosis victim, she was a refugee in England during World War II and died in 1943 as a result of refusing more food than was given those under Nazi rule. In her writings Christ is seen in this role (Tomlin 1954). However, when we speak of a martyr we can speak of one who does not pass on suffering that naturally comes his way, and another sort of martyr who somehow attracts to himself suffering from several sources which would not have otherwise affected him. For instance, Weil's refusal of food was not necessary in England. She was attempting to be a martyr of the second sort. Without discussing the merits of such an idea, how one goes about affecting such a transfer for therapeutic purposes is very poorly understood. On occasion a worried therapist appears to accept the burden and is himself the martyr. Clergymen frequently report being burdened as an occupational hazard.

Suicide in most cases does not terminate suffering. In fact, it transfers and magnifies suffering and, in spite of the need for treatment for someone who is depressed, often qualifies as the pentultimate evil act. In certain other cultures, *ritual* suicide (and martyrdom) may prevent a family from suffering pain, but in Western culture suicide generally entails the transfer and amplification of suffering and is not a ceremony or ritual.

If someone is "banished to the wilderness" following a symptom transfer, he is unable to pass on suffering. Perhaps our contemporary wilderness is the mental hospital.

ANIMALS AS SACRIFICES AND SCAPEGOATS

If symptoms or suffering could be transferred to an animal who is then banished or sacrificed, the individual or group may experience relief. This seems to happen without ceremony in certain families. Animal pets living with families sometimes share in the family problems. Speck (1965) reports that the members of one family were all suffering from a fear of leaving their house, and so were their cat and dog. He notes further:

In our work with psychotic families, pets are regularly in the session, since we hold the therapeutic sessions in the family's home. The pets often seem to reflect the feelings of the family members. For instance, if the family is friendly, the pet's behavior tends to be friendly also. It is not uncommon for pets to become ill in the family when significant human members of the family become ill. In psychotic families when aggression and behavioral disturbance becomes of high order, it is not unusual to see a cherished pet become ill, get injured, or get killed. This is usually followed by a period of mourning within the family and a marked lessening of the aggression and behavioral disturbance (Speck 1965, p. 226).

Similar use of animals has occurred ceremonially. The ancient Mosaic ritual of the Day of Atonement involved *two* goats, one of which was said to belong to the Lord and was sacrificed, ostensibly to "return" to him, and the other of which was sent out into the wilderness, to "e-scape," with the sins of the people laid on it, like an emissary—someone who is "emitted" from a closed system. The term "scapegoat" was coined by Tindale in 1530 to express literally the meaning of a Hebrew phrase occurring only in Leviticus 16:8, 10, 26 ("the goat on which the lot fell to scape"). Since "scape" is not used as a separate word, it has unfortunately made the term "scapegoat" lose any connotations which "escaping" might have imparted to it. It was rendered in Latin in the Vulgate *caper emissarius* and in French *buoc emissaire*, emphasizing the emitting or emissary aspects of the term.

If we use the term "scapegoat" properly, it should be

restricted to an animal to whom suffering is transferred and who is then banished, isolated, or ostracized. This is probably rarely done, but perhaps buying a pet and then abandoning it would be an example. I knew of an instance where a mother used to bring home or allow her children to bring home pets, usually dogs. Periodically she would say that she was taking the dog for a ride with her and return without the pet, who was never seen again. This would occur only after the pet had become one of the family. The children would be despondent and the mother somewhat more relaxed and warm toward them afterward. In this family the mother managed to dispose of four dogs, two sets of ducks, five or six cats, and almost succeeded with a horse before it could be rescued. Clearly the animals were serving some outlet function for the mother. She also became drunk and homicidal one evening, obtained a knife from the kitchen, and tried to kill her two youngest children. An older child found out and rescued the threatened children, who climbed out a window and spent the night in the park.

The Puerto Rican spiritualist in New York City is occasionally called upon to sacrifice an animal ceremonially. In this case we have a modern-day therapeutic ceremony. I once interviewed a man of about fifty married to a considerably younger woman. The husband had rather severe emphysema, and, perhaps, this influenced his potency. His original complaint was that his wife was being influenced by someone to become a whore. He consulted a spiritualist, who convened a ceremony at which both husband and wife were present and during which she sacrificed a chicken. The husband reported that suddenly he no longer felt angry, the wife was relieved, and, at the time of my interview, the husband claimed that "they" had not been bothered for approximately two years. Circumstances prevented my asking about potency changes.

In the case of a ceremonial sacrifice or scapegoating, the first task is to make the animal part of the family or the community. Humans to be sacrificed were often treated very well for a year in advance. The second task is to make the ceremonial act of scapegoating or sacrifice something beyond abuse or cruelty, and the third is to transfer to the animal the required suffering— proof of which is immediate relief on the part of the celebrants. These tasks are not as difficult as they may seem.

It is obviously beyond the scope and intentions of this chapter to coach the reader in the techniques of animal sacrifices. It is my view that we are dealing with a capacity that is inherent in the sacrificial situation, and probably very little in the way of ceremony is necessary if the natural conditions are available. Speck's simple expedient of prescribing a pet dog which he secretly suspects may be sacrificed is probably all that is necessary if the conditions are right; if they are not, there is probably little that can be done. However, if one reviews the literature of sacrifices that are not covertly arranged, it appears that every detail of the situation was made special: the place, the time, the sacrificer, the sacrificed, and so on. Care was taken to mystify the proceedings. For instance, in ancient Greece the ceremonial attendants accused each other of sacrificing the animal (or person), and finally the knife was blamed and thrown into the sea. Hubert and Mauss (1953) have reviewed the worldwide conditions for such ceremonies.

PHYSICAL PAIN—THE CATHARTIC METHOD

In several cases I have seen the following circumstances occurring. The patient met with some social misfortune and was miserable. During this period a serious pain syndrome developed, frequently a severe stomach disorder with painful cramps which may or may not have been induced by tension. The patients noticed that when the stomach cramps left, so did their feelings of misery. However, the precipitating social circumstances were unchanged. They still had the identical misfortune, but their suffering from it seemed to have left them along with their physical pain.

These observations bring to mind the ancient Greek and

Roman *method* of catharsis (which must be distinguished from
the modern *theory* of abreaction and cartharsis). The ancient
method actually involved catharsis in the literal sense. Patients
were given powerful purgatives or laxatives which must have
created severe stomach disorders, with cramps and diarrhea.
Then they were allowed to recover. Presumably there were
sufficient numbers of patients who found that, when the induced
suffering went away, so did the original misery.

SYMPTOM SHARING
AND THE TRANSFER OF HAPPINESS

Suffering can be transferred in its entirety or it can be shared
between different people, in which case only a part of the suffering is transferred. The mourning process seems to fit this model.
A large number of people convene and participate with those
hardest hit by the loss. As a result the suffering is diminished by
virtue of its having been divided and shared.

Not only can suffering be shared, but symptoms can be
shared as well. In what has come to be called "folie à deux,"
two people share a delusion. The term "folie communiquee,"
introduced by Laseque and Falret (1877) at the same time they
coined the term "folie à deux," seems a better label since it is
broader in scope. Classically, the condition involves two people
in close association, one of whom is dominant and has a delu-
sional idea. In tracing the history of the subject two tendencies
can be observed. One defines a distinct pathological entity, and
the other, more congruent with the ideas expressed above, considers spread, infection, contagion, and communication as central processes common to several pathological conditions.

Ending our illustrations on a more cheerful note, it might be
added that happiness, like suffering, can be transferred or

shared. In this context sharing is the preferred transaction, since more people are able to participate in the pleasure. However, there are occasions when a pleased or happy feeling is "transferred," appearing to leave one person and go to another. For example, a child comes home from school with an honor. His parents brag to their friends about the honor that their child has been accorded in such a fashion that the child feels as if he, himself, has been deprived of it.

Jealousy can be defined as failure of the sharing of happiness. To resent a competitor, which is often incorrectly identified as jealousy, is poor sportsmanship, perhaps, but not the same as feeling that someone who is close to you and who is experiencing happiness is somehow diminishing your pleasure. This latter phenomenon is more deserving of the special opprobrium associated with the term "jealousy."

While concern about symptom substitution has impeded the direct attack on symptoms, symptom substitution is also one of the oldest methods of treatment if we include with it symptom transfer, symptom sharing, and the transformation of symptoms (substitution and transfer). Psychoanalytic method is, perhaps, based on it. For example, Bruch is quoted as saying of anorexia nervosa that "a psychotherapeutic approach, with focus on the underlying personality structure, *deemphasizing the psychological importance of non-eating*, is often accompanied by resumption of normal eating in many previously inaccessible patients" (italics mine) (Bruch 1975, p. 8).

The phenomena of symptom transfer and transformation alert us to the possibility that the patient who asks for relief might be coming to the therapist as a result of bearing someone else's suffering. Furthermore, he may "dump" this worry on the therapist. While this seldom occurs to psychotherapists, or so we would like to believe, it is apparently more common with clergymen, who often find their lives quite stressful as a result of their role as *proxies*, or as martyrs.

Whereas symptom substitution both worried psychotherapists

and was often their main technical device, symptom transfer has been largely neglected by them (with the exceptions of certain family therapists), although it has been widely employed in folk magic and ceremonies. Recognition of the pervasiveness of symptom substitution, transfer, and sharing can lead to new therapeutic strategies, greater diagnostic sophistication, and better understanding of folk medicine and folk psychiatry. It can build a bridge from our field to ethics (Rabkin 1972). The growing realization that symptom removal is not likely to be followed by symptom substitution should not be allowed to obscure this fascinating area of study.

CHAPTER 8

Disturbed and Disturbing: Therapy for More Than One Person at a Time

PROBLEMS related to marriage or family have been identified as the antecedent event motivating approximately half of those who seek outpatient psychotherapy. A survey by Sager and colleagues (1968) demonstrated that 50 percent of the patients requesting psychotherapy did so largely because of marital difficulties, and another 25 percent had problems related to marriage. Gurin and colleagues (1960) found similar results in a nationwide survey in which marital concerns ranked first and other family problems followed as the major reasons for seeking help with emotional problems. Psychodynamic psychotherapy, with its emphasis on the personal and developmental aspects of an individual's life, is difficult to adapt to such problems. As a result, they are frequently redefined. However, strategic psychotherapy can easily be modified so that the therapist can see more than one person at a time if they are members of the same natural group—a marriage, a family, or a network—and can approach the problem as it is presented without redefinition.

Strategic psychotherapy with more than one person at a time

falls into three different categories. These are marital and family psychotherapy, crisis intervention, and what might be called clinical epistemology, encompassing the investigation and treatment of many conditions formerly seen as individual problems from a transactional point of view. Depression, paranoia, and dying are considered in this context. An attempt will be made to show that not only are we dealing with an individual who is disturbed but one who is disturbing to his environment.

MARITAL AND FAMILY THERAPY

When a patient seeks psychotherapy with a primary complaint about a family or marriage, one possible treatment strategy is to observe the entire family or marital interaction in your office or in their home. The purpose of such observation is to determine the prevailing family methods of solving problems, in order to modify and make them more effective. This is most clearly apparent in behavioral approaches to marriage therapy, where most investigators report that the families they have seen rely excessively on punitive measures to influence each other's behavior (Jacobson and Martin 1976). The result is either reciprocal use of such aversive tactics or withdrawal from contact with each other, accompanied by progressive decline of good feelings toward each other and the marriage. The therapist's task is to develop intervention strategies that modify this interaction pattern, first by identifying what it is, then bringing it to the attention of husband and wife, and eventually teaching them more effective ways of dealing with each other.

Almost all that has been said about strategies with the individual patient can apply to the treatment of his marriage or family as well. For example, a patient can have a marital problem about which he is demoralized but his wife is still optimistic.

He enters therapy when his wife finally becomes demoralized as well, and her positive feelings no longer counteract the patient's negative ones. Treatment in such a case must affect the wife as well as the husband, although it may be possible to see only one. The wife's hopefulness may be revived from knowing that her husband has finally sought professional help. The problem of morale can also be approached by seeing them together. In general, the tasks of conjoint therapy, seeing more than one person at a time, are the same as those of individual therapy. Complaints must be pinpointed and plausible and acceptable goals established. The charge that "you are always trying to hurt me" is an impossible problem to treat successfully. On the other hand, "You criticized my driving in front of Lois and Fred" is much more manageable (Jacobson and Martin 1976).

The opening phase of family or marital therapy is similar in most respects to that of individual therapy. There are, however, two problems that should be discussed: secrets, and gathering together the proper group for treatment. If the therapist becomes privy to a secret (for example, that the patient has a mistress who his wife believes he gave up several months before), he is placed in a particularly poor position to see the couple together. The only solution is to make clear that you will not keep secrets. Most patients will accept this even after they have told you such a secret. I would hasten to explain that there is a difference between divulging "raw data" which the other spouse would not comprehend, such as the contents of a dream, and utilizing its interpretation. For example, if a husband dreams that he is making love to his wife's best friend, I do not regard this as a secret that must be divulged. On the other hand, it is worth considering what prompted such a dream. If it suggests that the couple have been too busy as parents and breadwinners to spend time with each other as husband and wife, and might benefit from a weekend alone while the grandparents take care of their children, *this* might profitably be discussed in the session.

The decision about whether or not to see more than one

person at a time depends upon the therapist's estimation of the system with which he is dealing, and where its boundaries lie. There are times when a distant acquaintance is responsible for considerable input into a social system, while a close relative is not. When I worked with eight-to-twelve-year-old delinquent boys, one of the remedial education students was a nun. She decided to acquaint herself with the environent from which one of the boys came. Dressed in her nun's habit, she visited the neighborhood with the child, who was very proud to show her off. One of the most important people he wanted her to meet was the local grocery store owner. When the grocer met the nun he whispered, "What a shame. Hector is such a nice boy, but you know what an alcoholic mother can do. . . ." The nun made an effort to correct this attitude right on the spot. She spent some time with the grocer, urging him to stop pitying the child and licensing his delinquent behavior on the grounds that he had no father and his mother neglected him. She got him to stop referring to the residential treatment center where the boy lived during the week as "that place," and persuaded him to ask the child how his reading was progressing each time he came to the store. Soon the grocer would ask him to read some of the labels on the food he came to buy. While not a family member, this man played a significant role in the boy's experience, and modifying his behavior directly influenced the boy.

Several midgame strategies have been developed to increase the use of positive reinforcement (rewards) and decrease an excessively high rate of punishment. Many of the approaches are educational. Alternative strategies are suggested, modeled, or role-played, and attempts to change tactics are monitored, sometimes using videotape feedback. Using "behavioral rehearsals," couples practice new strategies while therapists monitor, encourage, and correct. Other approaches suggest contingency management procedures with the use of written contracts in which a quid pro quo (this for that) is outlined. A contract has disadvantages in practice because it sanctions one member to stop if the other does. An alternative is for each member of a family or couple to learn a list of reinforcers and methods which they apply independently. It is also helpful to pick target behavior that one wants to increase in frequency rather than decrease, since these tasks are easier to accomplish. Token economies have been used to help make tasks concrete in the homes of distressed couples.

When observing a family or couple in action, other problems have been delineated. For example, Minuchin and Bowen both have emphasized that in certain families the individuals are too involved with each other. Minuchin (1974) refers to this as "enmeshment" and Bowen (1966) as "fusion." In these families, although punishment may be used excessively, it is frequently in situations which didn't warrant concern in the first place. "Benign neglect" would be better. One colleague described growing up in such a family: when he did not eat, he thought his mother would lose weight! From a systems point of view, such families are too richly interconnected, and therapy consists of attempting to correct this. For example, children should not have to put on sweaters when their mother is cold. Time spent alone or away from the family, physical privacy, and involvement in activities with nonfamily members are helpful corrective strategies. Minuchin and colleagues (1967) have also described the converse in which some families, particularly lower-class ones, do not have enough interconnections.

A strategy of beign neglect depends for it effectiveness on the reward and punishment contingencies in the world outside of the family. Enmeshed or fused families are overly concerned with each other because there is no reliance on the community, sometimes rightfully so. A too richly interconnected system is another way of saying that the system has too impermeable a boundary. By choosing which private school a child attends, by arranging for specific extracurricular experiences such as summer camp and music lessons, families that have the financial resources, social rank, and social effectiveness can maintain executive control and shape their destinies and those of their children with a strategy of apparent benign neglect because the contingencies in the restricted universe in which the family lives are such that certain values will be upheld. However, when this state of events does not prevail, because the family's values are eccentric or because the community is inferior, or its own boundary cannot withstand the onslaughts of the media or some other outside influence, or when a family does not have the necessary financial resources and organizational skills, one of two possibilities will occur: either enmeshment or fusion as the family members attempt to be all things to everyone, or complete collapse of the boundary and the community invasion of the family territory, destroying the interconnectedness necessary for family life. There is a delicate balance necessary between family and community; when this is upset, the effects can be noticed within the family. I think that we tend to be too critical of certain parental concerns which seem stereotypically neurotic. It is not appropriate to place the blame on the family itself for its lack of status or its unfavorable environment.

Another observation that has been made about families and couples is that those in distress do not freely communicate their opinions and feelings. In general this has been incorporated into the treatment strategies subsumed under assertiveness training. The patients are taught how to "confront" rather than "attack" each other. If the subject sticks to a statement about himself ("I am unhappy") rather than statements about the other person ("You are hostile"), an assertive rather than an aggressive or violent statement can be made. "I wish I could believe that" is much better than "You are a liar."

Finally, decision-making patterns have been the focus of midgame strategies. Distressed couples tend to display ambiguous, ineffective, and even chaotic decision-making patterns. Training is required in such cases to develop a well-working system. In other families a leader-follower pattern, a competitive pattern, a cooperative pattern, or some mixture of these may be responsible for distress. For example, a cooperative pattern based on a fear of conflict (the "Yes-dear" type of response) can lead to considerable discomfort in the submissive partner. The so-called "perfect marriage" in which there are never fights can benefit from "fight training." Competitive relationships can be alive and "spunky," but at times they may become so competitive that the individuals are permanent adversaries. Under these circumstances child rearing, breadwinning, and sex are seen in a win-lose framework. In a leader-follower relationship an excessive dominant-submissive pattern can develop. The task of the therapist frequently is to modify rather than change such relationships. For example, cooperation that is not based on fear of conflict might be the goal of therapy with an overly cooperative "perfect" marriage (Ravich and Wyden 1974).

MORE THAN ONE THERAPIST AT A TIME

Multiproblem families are often sent to several agencies simultaneously, each of which works with a piece of the problem. In one case that I was acquainted with, a family was involved with seventeen agencies. In another situation I was asked to see a couple, each of whom had a therapist. They had a child who also had a therapist. While there are many aspects to such therapy, the outstanding issue is its coordination. In order to deal with such situations, Auerswald (1971) developed a conference format in which all the therapists attend with all their supervisors. The entire family is placed on one side of a one-way mirror, with the therapists on the other. It is best if the family performs some concrete task, but an interview will suffice. After the entire group has had an opportunity to see a specific sample of behavior of the entire social group in treatment, the case is discussed. It is hoped that some coordinated program will be developed and a "chairman of the case" appointed whose job it is to keep everyone informed, keep the pace of problem solving going, and make sure that a certain modicum of spirit and morale exists in the treatment group.

CRISIS INTERVENTION

Crisis intervention is another area in which strategies have been developed for more than one person at a time. Unfortunately, a polarization of opinion has developed, with the antipsychiatry forces arguing on one side that there are no individual problems, only environmental ones, and the so-called "medical model" advocates on the other side who focus their attention exclusively upon the mind or brain.

The concept of crisis is closely linked to that of stress, which has received considerably more attention among natural and social scientists, both theoretically and in terms of animal and human research. A crisis or emergency, as the terms are used here, entails an abrupt change in ongoing behavioral patterns, usually precipitated by an event or social change that is perceived by the individual as potentially threatening. A crisis is simply a change in a steady state which may or may not warrant intervention; an emergency unequivocally requires it. While there are some extreme environmental conditions that constitute severe stressors for all who are exposed, as in the case of natural disasters such as floods or man-made disasters such as concentration camps, in the vast majority of situations the impact of stressful events is mediated both by characteristics and attributes of the individual, and by the degree of protection he has available in terms of social support systems. What constitutes an acutely stressful event for an individual thus depends on the severity of the event, his personal attributes, and his social network. Those with certain biological predispositions or social attributes may be more vulnerable to stressful events than others, as are those who lack social ties or any form of group membership.

Considering the first component in this stress formula—the experience or event—a variety of situations have been identified by social scientists as normal growth crises which occur with fairly predictable regularity at specified transition points in the family and life cycle. These include marriage, birth of a child, job promotion, and other life events associated with role alterations. For the growing child, going away to school or death of a parent constitute normal growth crises.

Although the impact of stressful situations is to some extent mediated by uniquely individual strengths, deficits, resources, talents, and relationships, some general patterns of response have been observed that facilitate therapeutic strategies in crisis situations. At such times the individual is more amenable to change at behavioral, attitudinal, and cognitive levels. Crisis investigators speak of a temporary fluidity of personality, a loosening of identity, which facilitates both adaptive and maladaptive behavioral change at such times. A crisis is therefore a time of opportunity—for the therapist, who has more leverage because of the patient's heightened compliance and susceptibility to influence, and for the patient, whose increased capacity to change behavior, attitude, and thought can lead to a completely new life.

A crisis is also a time of risk. The very features characterizing the individual in crisis are apt to be construed by those who meet him for the first time during this interval as signs of weakness or pathology. This is especially possible if such an individual is separated from former friends and relatives and is presently isolated. Since identity is fluid at these times and the individual's resources are depleted, the appraisals of others during the crisis are apt to be less flattering than those of one's usual associates. They are also likely to be accepted by the person undergoing the crisis as valid predictive statements.

When a person in crisis comes into contact with a mental health professional, two very different outcomes are possible. Traditionally, the crisis behavior was interpreted as symptomatic of an ongoing pathological process; the person was diagnosed as mentally ill, separated from his family and friends if he had managed to maintain these relationships up to this time, extracted from his neighborhood, and sent to a distant mental hospital. In this context, the nineteenth-century psychiatric title of "alienist" seems appropriate. In this approach the individual's identity becomes that of mental patient, with all the social stigma and incapacity the label implies.

A different construction can be applied by mental health professionals in dealing with a person in crisis. Instead of viewing the person as suffering from a disease, Virchow's view of disease as "life under altered conditions" (in Menninger 1963, p. 41) may be evoked. The individual can often be supported in his usual setting, his social ties reinforced instead of severed, and a problem-solving perspective applied. The public will usually tolerate considerable deviance as long as it is not labeled "mental illness." Similarly, most families will cooperate with the therapist in dealing with the upsets associated with a crisis experience. It is thus often socially feasible, economically efficient, and therapeutically effective to sidestep the label of mental illness and focus on reinforcing or developing socially adaptive behavior in the individual in crisis. At the same time, one can make sure that the person in crisis and those around him retain an image of the subject's identity before the crisis, with the implication that the patient will return to this state.

An example of the application of this approach is embodied in the work of Soteria House, which serves as a community alternative to psychiatric hospitalization. Soteria House, in California, is operated as a boarding house where schizophrenic patients live for a period of approximately five months with young staff members who are chosen in part on the basis of their nonmedical attitudes. Taught to adopt a positive view of schizophrenia, the staff members are encouraged to tolerate unusual behavior and to "accept" the psychotic experience as a "valid" one. The underlying philosophy of Soteria House and other antipsychiatric programs explicitly rejects the medical model in the management of schizophrenia. Mosher (1976), one of the sponsors of Soteria House, views hospitalization for acute schizophrenia as producing a cycle of spiraling negative expectations which is more likely to create chronic patients than to produce recovery.

Any theoretical framework serves to influence the expectations of the therapist and in turn the patient, whether it is transactional or existential. Varieties of antipsychiatric theory indirectly maintain that psychosis is an interpersonal game played by the clever patient against his family, or, alternatively, that psychosis is a valuable state of self-confrontation, better than normality as the path to real sanity (Laing 1960). The particular antipsychiatric theory espoused by Mosher, Laing, and others has as its major practical effect avoidance of the label and role assignment of mental patient. The professional and family members surrounding the individual in crisis are manipulated into roles that avoid assignment of stigma, predictions of chronicity, or removal of the patient from his social network.

While these outcomes are estimable, the question arises whether this convoluted philosophical approach is the most direct method available to achieve them. It would seem that the strategic therapist has recourse to a variety of techniques which will produce the same outcomes, without need for the accompanying theoretical antipsychiatry bias. Hansell's work (1976) is an excellent example.

The three components of a stressful situation that determine its impact on the individual—the dimensions of the environmental event, the individual's personal resources, and the nature of his social support system—can each be managed in most instances by the strategic therapist. Some stressful events can be modified by the therapist's intervention, as when a runaway adolescent needs aid in negotiating his return home, or, more commonly, the therapeutic efforts can be addressed to bolstering the individual's personal resources, competencies, and social supports.

Social isolation is a major factor in the evolution of psychiatric disorders, medical illnesses, and even premature mortality. It has been found that adults who live alone, with no meaningful social relationships or group ties, have higher rates of mental illness, alcoholism, tuberculosis, and mortality from virtually all causes than do fellow citizens of the same age who are involved in their families, communities, or some other meaningful social network. Isolation is thus a hazardous predisposing factor, increasing vulnerability to stress and illness. It is also a feared outcome of a crisis that the individual will lose membership in his group. In a crisis situation the therapist can intervene to protect or strengthen social ties. One strategy that has been developed by Speck and Attneave (1971) is to convene the individual's entire social network to rally support and continued acceptance. If there is no network to convene, a program can be worked out to involve the individual in a group with some shared interest. Hansell (1976) has published a manual of such techniques, reviewing several varieties of self-help groups designed to meet this problem. He has also discussed the necessity for dealing with the patient's network to prevent unnecessary chronicity. In contrast to Speck and Attneave, who are willing to convene upwards of a hundred people, Hansell feels that three or four key persons may be all that is necessary.

The focus on the network's reaction to a person in distress is often merely another way of describing family or marriage therapy. In these cases the person in distress is not displaying flagrant "crisis plumage," a term of Hansell's (1976). However, many of the same processes and concerns can be distinguished. For example, a child who refuses to attend school can be labeled much the same way that a person in crisis can be labeled. He can be attached to a helping network or else he can be stigmatized. In the latter case the school might insist that the child see a psychiatrist to cure his symptom, which might be viewed as a manifestation of more enduring pathology requiring extended treatment. Alternatively, he could be treated by a therapist who has seen several young children who have refused to do things, such as swimming at camp or wearing anything but blue clothes, and who does not view this event as anything more than one of the crises one usually meets in life. Such a therapist might work with the family and school to solve the specific problem of school attendance. The approach is similar to the Soteria method described above, but without the philosophy.

In family therapy one often hears the remark that the family rather than the patient is sick, that it is a schizophrenic family rather than a family with an individual who has a schizophrenic reaction to stress. This serves the function for the therapist, and for the family if they agree with him, of not extruding the patient or labeling him mentally ill. However, to refer the problem to the marriage or family can sometimes not solve the problem at the level. For example, if a child has a school phobia, already labeled, it is hard to see the point of saying that there must be something wrong with his parents' marriage, too. Compliant and intelligent parents will then start to reexamine their relationship in terms of a hypothetical normal and correct way of living. They will reframe their behavior now as something pathological. Let us assume for purpose of illustration that they have a leader-follower pattern of decision making (as do approximately 25 percent of couples in the United States [Ravich and Wyden 1975]). Now that their child has a "disease" called school phobia, and a person in authority has laid the blame on their marriage, they are likely to reevaluate as bad or sick that which has been a working pattern for them. Just as the label "mental illness" can itself lead to certain actions, so can the diagnosis of a bad marriage. In a parallel sense the "identity" of a marriage is fluid in times of crisis, and the reaction or expectations of the therapist has an influence on the outcome. Some couples and families need to be told that they have a healthy marriage, that their behavior during a crisis is not all there is to their relationship. They have to be referred back to times when things were going well and to the future when this will be repeated.

Crisis intervention attempts to develop a tripartite strategy that eliminates or modifies hazardous stressors, strengthens the individual's ability to undergo stress, and supports the buffering, anchoring, and repairing instituted by the social network. In the first and third areas others besides the identified patient must be dealt with clinically.

TRANSACTIONAL ANALYSIS OF INDIVIDUAL SYMPTOMS: CLINICAL EPISTEMOLOGY

Both depressed and paranoid patients often complain about the unfriendly behavior of other people in their social environments. Traditionally, such complaints have been regarded as distortions and misperceptions, and hence evidence of mental illness. However, it has been demonstrated that the natural groups surrounding such patients do indeed act in ways that match the patient's critical appraisals of them. The patient has probably played a major role in bringing about the rejection and hostility in the case of depression, or the conspiracy in the case of paranoia, but once such patterns have emerged, they tend to assume autonomy and can be observed by the clinician. In this section emphasis will be placed on the transactional rather than personal aspects of these conditions, although the latter are most certainly integral components. Many, perhaps all, functional psychiatric conditions could serve as illustrations of this transactional process. I have chosen to discuss depression and paranoia in some detail because an extensive description is needed to counteract the tendency to regard these conditions as located exclusively within the individual. Analysis of the transactional aspects of individual mental problems is, perhaps, strategic psychotherapy's most distinctive aspect. At the same time, such discussion becomes rather complicated, bordering on the philosophical.

The most vivid metaphor for the pernicious process to be described is that the depressed or paranoid patient and his immediate associates and next of kin are locked into an inflexible and stereotyped relationship which progressively and inexorably "drifts" toward extreme states and disaster for all. People seldom acknowledge their negative responses to depressed and paranoid patients. The psychiatric literature looks, at times as if its authors are willing partners to such denial. The depressed patient is described as unresponsive to the "support surrounding him" and the paranoid is said to complain of a "pseudocommunity" which conspires against him. In fact, there is considerable validity to allegations of hostility toward patients with both conditions, although people obviously have positive feelings as well, or else they wouldn't have anything to do with these disturbed and disturbing, troubled and troublesome people.

Like members of their social networks, therapists also have their difficulties in dealing with depressed and paranoid patients. Cohen (Cohen et al. 1954) found that therapists, like others in their environment, react to depressive manipulations with unrealistic assurances and "seductive promises too great to be fulfilled." When the patient believes these promises and tries to realize them, the therapist responds with hostility and efforts at disengagement. Even this is denied, however, and covered over with platitudes addressed to the patient: such behavioral response ultimately qualifies as countermanipulation that can leave everyone involved depressed, guilty, and responding cruelly to each other (Fromm-Reichman 1959; Jacobson 1954). It reduces pleasurable input drastically.

In an interesting experiment, Coyne (1976) arranged for naive subjects to talk on the telephone for twenty minutes at a time to members of each of three groups: normal people, depressed patients, and other patients attending a psychiatric clinic. His subjects responded to the depressed patients with unrealistic reassurance and useless advice. They were likely to

feel depressed, anxious, and angry during and after their contacts with the depressed patients, although they did not let the
patients know this. In addition, they rejected further opportuni-
ties to speak with the depressed patients, but not with the other
groups. As we shall see, a similar process occurs with paranoid
patients.

DEPRESSION: THE MIDAS STORY

Depressions are characteristically associated with the experience of loss, either of a social role, an important relationship, an
anticipated goal, or any combination of these events. Such losses
are often irreversible, as in the case of widowhood, although
adjustments, compromises, and substitutions are certainly feasible. Unlike others who manage to reach a satisfactory adjustment, the depressed patient has failed to do so; his "restorative"
strategies are not effective. In many instances his behavior
comes to be seen as manipulative and insensitive to the efforts
of others by those who deal with him. Lewinsohn (1975) has
identified three predisposing characteristics of those who become
depressed: they are socially inept, yet they prefer social rein-
forcements to any other kind, and they have difficulty delaying
gratification. Following a loss, they discover the Midas-like
effects of "depressing" at others (to be described in detail below).
They cannot delay efforts at restitution and so are intent upon
utilizing such techniques. By the time this process has begun
they do not seem warmly disposed toward others, not direct or
intimate, and they give the impression of being manipulative.
Although they achieve their aim of restitution beyond their
wildest dreams, they are eventually in serious trouble, like
Midas in the legend, because of it.

To refer to a depressed patient as "manipulative" or deficient
in warmth and concern for others is incorrect, not because the
description is inaccurate, but because it implies that an origin or
beginning of events has been found within the individual. When
one believes that he has found the beginning of a chain of

events, it is customary to place the responsibility there, a process which may culminate in the phenomenon Ryan (1971) has called "blaming the victim." On the other hand, to imply that a depressed patient bears no responsibility for his predicament would be equally misleading.

Depression can be classified into three phases. In the first phase the person in distress emits a series of messages (expressions of helplessness, hopelessness, withdrawal, agitation) which tend to engage others immediately. These distress signals usually cause those in his social network to gather around the person in distress, with the effect of shifting the burden of restoration to these other people. Depressions occur in situations in which immediate restoration is impossible, yet the distressed individual cannot tolerate its delay.

Those who are the recipients of the depressive's pleas often cannot help despite their good intentions. For example, the new widow usually suffers a decline in social status, and sometimes in financial security as well. She no longer receives the invitations to the social gatherings and business conventions that formerly depended on her husband's status or occupation. Relatives and friends may do their best to include the widow in their own activities, but they cannot restore her social standing in the larger community or arrange for her remarriage. Their failure to do so leads to escalated expressions of distress which provoke renewed assurances and well-meaning but implausible suggestions from friends and family. The persistence and repetition of these distress signals, which come to be seen as symptoms, is both incomprehensible and objectionable to others.

Part of the aversive aspect of such transactions lies in the demanding quality of the distress signals, but part of the pain of dealing with such a person is prompted by exposure of flaws in the social fabric that such a situation reveals. Irritated and increasingly guilt ridden, members of the social network continue to give reassurances, but faint clues suggest that these have become formulas. The depressive begins to suspect, with some justice, that he is not really accepted any more, that he is being given charity. Others begin to avoid him, and most transactions are up to him to initiate. Often everyone feels guilty and unhappy. Certain essential input is thus lacking for the depressive. And this is probably critical as an etiological factor.

Phase two of the depressive reaction now evolves as social group and patient become locked into their respective roles. Even if the patient now makes an honest attempt to find out what is wrong, such efforts would be indistinguishable from his previous strategy to those with whom he is interacting. Eventually the problem escalates as the patient shifts to a sick role in an effort to escape the pattern and appeal to a wider audience. Now his behavior is more confusing and difficult than ever for his friends and relatives to handle, and they withdraw further.

The final phase is characterized by the patient's increasing his symptoms and complaining of being worthless, guilty, or evil, the classic self-accusations of the depressed mental patient. He displays these symptoms aggressively, which baffles those to whom they are addressed, since people who actually feel that way would be unlikely to advertise it. The audience widens to include mental health professionals and the messages become more obscure and perplexing. At this point hospitalization is a probable outcome.

Depressed patients have many problems of an individual and even biochemical nature, but these occurrences do not fully explain the environment's response to them. Coyne (1976) reports a case illustration in which the therapist had attempted to treat her patient's complaints of worthlessness with explicit reassurances that she more than understood and cared for her, she *loved* her. After weeks of such reassurance and increasingly frequent sessions, the patient suggested they spend the night together. At this point the therapist attempted to terminate the relationship so that the patient could "apply her insights gained in therapy to her daily life." However, the patient continued to appear for sessions and made vague suicidal gestures. When

Coyne suggested to the therapist that she confront the patient honestly, the therapist refused on the grounds that she truly loved the patient and would do nothing to hurt her!

Therapists familiar with depressed patients read this sort of transcript and sigh, "There but for the grace of God . . ." recognizing the risks and perils of such cases. A colleague, now a senior faculty member, began treating a depressed woman when he was still a resident. Many years later she took a trip. To see her off at the airport were only my colleague (her psychiatrist) and her internist. Both were rather puzzled and amazed at how they, busy professionals, found themselves in such a situation. I would like to suggest that part of the answer to this puzzle lies in the fact that neither the psychiatrist nor the internist wished to be reminded that there are people in this world about whom everybody ceases to care. The depressive to some minor degree is a threat to our illusions. If we turn to paranoia, another more generally acknowledged threat, we can see the same theme more highly developed.

PARANOIA: THE EMPEROR'S NEW CLOTHES

While the depressive attempts to regain lost ground in a plaintive fashion, the paranoid, in vivid contrast, tries to do so in a bold, often cruel and outrageous fashion. Bizarre and unsuccessful paranoia, like the bizarre and unsuccessful final stages of depression, is often the standard for psychiatric diagnosis, but there are also less flagrant and relatively more effective varieties observable among those who are not identified as mentally ill. In this presentation the "successful" paranoid is discussed first.

The Successful Paranoid.   In general, a hallmark of the paranoid strategy is disregard for the subtle, unwritten rules for attaining status, reform, or promotion, together with exclusive reliance on one's own perceptions rather than group consensus. The paranoid's conviction of what is right and wrong, even what is real or unreal, is based on his personal judgment rather than on feedback from others. He is like the boy in the fairytale of

"The Emperor's New Clothes" who sees that the Emperor is naked. This is not due to his greater wisdom, but to the total autonomy of his perceptions and his insensitivity to social consensus. The paranoid may also be the "honest" policeman in a corrupt department who betrays the confidences he has obtained, sticks to the rulebook, and obeys the written codes rather than the informal one. If his judgment happens to be accurate, he may successfully trigger a reform movement.

Paranoids are often intimidating to their subordinates in social or occupational settings. They will relentlessly attack those who are defenseless in the name of the truth, the right, or the rulebook. They are difficult, brash, irritating, and often thoroughly unlikable. However, they can, at their best, initiate or work for militant social reforms and articulate genuine social dissatisfactions.

The paranoid's ability to provoke atypical behavior in others is illustrated by the actions of a prominent lecturer who is a concentration camp survivor. He believes that he is being persecuted by the secret police of the countries where he travels. As a consequence, he carries chained to his arm a briefcase containing his essential papers. Since he frequently travels internationally to give lectures, he takes certain precautions which appear logical, given his beliefs and past experiences. He arrives at airports early so that, if he is investigated, he will still make his departure time. With his briefcase chained to his arm, checking and rechecking his passport continually, and glancing furtively around him, he sits alone on a bench. This behavior is almost certain to attract the attention of security police, who then question him. This substantiates his belief that he is being followed and persecuted by the police, and increases his wariness.

The paranoid's success lies in the skill with which he can provoke a damaging reaction. The psychiatric nurse who wants to get rid of a disagreeable patient on her ward, but cannot manage to do so through proper channels, may place a small paper cup containing strong-smelling paraldehyde *above* the patient's *upper* lip and then spill it toward his nose. He pushes her away while she vigorously persists until she can yell for help on the grounds that she is being assaulted. The patient, beside himself with rage at being so duped, is removed to the violent ward in restraints, *appropriately* because he is now actually violent. The paranoid, however, is the nurse.

The Paranoid as Mental Patient. Not all paranoid maneuvers are successful. It is, in fact, the rare exception who can effectively bring about social reforms, uncover corruption, and win recognition as a leader with a devoted following. Most of the time the paranoid is met with doubt developing into incredulity. He may be perceived as a crackpot or a crank. Not only does he fail to win power in a group situation, but he is often excluded from its informal processes and networks.

In a work situation the paranoid individual may make his superiors uncomfortable with his obsequiousness, and his colleagues irritated with his social insensitivity, obliviousness to the spirit rather than the letter of procedures and regulations, and lack of warmth, trust, and friendliness. In reaction, they may share their discomfort about him with each other, huddling around the water cooler to discuss the problem. They may even have a prearranged signal, such as the theme from *Dragnet,* to warn of his approach. The paranoid may see the cluster of colleagues whispering in a conspiratorial manner, and he may hear the *Dragnet* theme as he comes near, but he is incapable of handling this complicated and difficult problem (Lemert 1962).

The paranoid individual flounders in such circumstances. His legalistic rulebook strategy does not apply to the subtle, unspoken, escalating group reaction. He becomes increasingly walled off from others, leading to two results, both ultimately serious. First, he is isolated in the midst of a group which depends on a high level of mutual trust and communication for fulfillment of its goals. A number of studies have suggested that such a condition in and of itself can precipitate severe stress reactions in those who have withstood other forms of stress quite well, such as the elderly, the deaf, and war victims who have become displaced persons. Second, the paranoid may experience an urgent need to succeed in this setting because of his past failures together with his perception of another impending rejection. In our society, each consecutive failure becomes more stigmatizing. One mistake is overlooked, two may be tolerated, but cumulative failures lead to exclusion, isolation, and a notorious reputation. The current situation is thus seen by the paranoid as hazardous, stressful, and ultimately unbearable (Lemert 1962).

At this point, "paranoid drift" occurs. As the two sides remain locked together in the struggle, the respective participants become increasingly fearful of each other and the relationship drifts to further polarization. Those who have to deal with the individual worry that some insane violence will occur, that he will explode. The paranoid might worry about the same thing. He resorts to increasingly incompetent efforts to provoke strong feelings and receive some kind of meaningful communication—not for the original purpose of personal advancement but to deal with isolation. He is threatening, insulting, blunt, legalistic. In order to clarify what is happening, he initiates a series of written communications. He notes obscure transactions, remarks, and behavior which seem to him to document his suspicions but which appear to others as exaggerations and incorrect interpretations. He keeps detailed records. But then so does the group trying to deal with him. The so-called "pseudocommunity" (like the hostility of the social network in response to depressives) can be shown to exist. This community is just as isolated from the subject as he is from them. Their fear of his physical dangerousness is not borne out by studies, although it is easy to see why such thoughts occur. He is a danger to the social fabric, or was originally, but not physically threatening to its members. However, his reputation is now as one who is a dangerous person. Ultimately, as Goffman (1961) has shown, he is literally betrayed into hospitalization.

A case presented to the New York County District Branch of

the American Psychiatric Association as an example of a difficult legal, clinical, and ethical crisis concerned a thirty-seven-year-old single, unemployed white female who acted strangely while delivering a child in a city hospital. The psychiatric consultant determined that she was in treatment with a private psychiatrist, whom he called without obtaining the patient's consent. This psychiatrist stated that she was paranoid and schizophrenic. The patient spoke, among other things, of being an agent for the FBI (false), suing the Small Business Administration for $40,000 (subsequently confirmed), and of her other children who were in placement. Without the patient's consent, the Bureau of Child Welfare was called; it was eventually decided not to give her custody of her infant on discharge. She sued the Bureau of Child Welfare for kidnapping, and the hospital psychiatrist and her private psychiatrist for breach of confidentiality (malpractice).

To the extent that she may have actually precipitated illegal behavior from which she may later benefit financially, she "succeeded" as a paranoid. It seems understandable that the hospital should be concerned, that one physician would call another, even that the private psychiatrist would say "She's really a crazy lady. Schizophrenic and paranoid as hell. . . ." It is even understandable that that remark would appear on her chart. However, it is understandable only in terms of the informal rules of operation, the common law, not the rulebooks. Ultimately, if this case is true to form, *informal*, behind-the-scenes court procedures will lead to this patient's losing her case. It will baffle her.

Although this woman may have been successful in catching the hospital off guard, she was unsuccessful in another larger sense. She had earlier sought private psychiatric care, we must remember. She did so because she was "nervous" and felt that people were looking at her "in a funny way." She had probably already been isolated. Although at the outset of this episode there was no gross evidence of thought disorder, by the end she was showing some loosening of associations. She created fear, and was herself frightened by the conspiracy which took her baby away for nefarious purposes by illegal means—what might they do next? She was further isolated.

The most pathetic interpretation of this case, which is admittedly conjectural, is that this woman wanted desperately to keep the baby, and in order to do so she concealed her past history. She was not identified by the hospital as a difficult patient until delivery. On the obstetrics floor she told nobody about her relatives, gave false identification of her welfare social worker, and made up a story about being an FBI agent to justify her behavior. This might have triggered the process that ultimately led to such a dismaying outcome.

A therapist has to help a paranoid obtain his goals. He has to stick to the rulebook. Hardest of all, he has to be willing to accept the fact that social consensus determines how we react, what we believe, and in the extreme case even what we "see." Piaget has said that "reality is a game we teach our children." The position that reality is a construct is presented in an informal way in a recent book by Watzlawick (1976). The transactional analysis of paranoia hinges on this idea. The paranoid hasn't learned to play this type of game, and those who have to deal with him often do not acknowledge that there is a game at all. In a sense there are two opposite problems: the paranoid who can't play games (in Piaget's sense of the word) and the antiparanoid who can play the game but can't see what it is. The therapist has to be willing and able both to play the game and to see that there is a game being played. He has the almost impossible task of admiring our emperor's new clothes and knowing that they do not exist independently of our social expectations.

DYING AND DENIAL

Once a network becomes aware that someone is dying, there is a tendency for its members to withdraw. Often the dying person is not told directly that he is expected to die, yet the behavior of those around him (their failure to make eye contact when they reassure him, for example) at the very least makes him suspicious. As in paranoia and depression, a hypocritical attitude is assumed toward him. Most dying persons are aware of their fate, most paranoids and depressives recognize the counterreaction, but in the social system around them they cannot feel free to reveal their knowledge. The "mutual pretense" becomes a burden. Everyone must act, in the case of the dying person, as if nothing is happening. Tolstoy described this state as follows:

> What tormented Ivan Illych most was the deception, the lie, which for some reason they all accepted, that he was not dying but was simply ill, and that he only need keep quiet and undergo a treatment and then something very good would result. He however knew that do what they would nothing would come of it, only still more agonizing suffering and death. This deception tortured him —their not wishing to admit what they all knew and what he knew, but wanting to lie to him concerning his terrible condition, and wishing and forcing him to participate in that lie (Tolstoy, p. 137).

Treatment techniques that prevent the development of mutual pretense in dying have now been developed. In fact, "hospices" designed for terminally ill patients to spend their last few weeks are now being introduced in the United States on an experimental basis. Group therapy on a ward where there are dying patients reduces the number of psychiatric consultations drastically.

The denial of death has other, longer-range consequences for the entire social fabric, hinted at in Tolstoy's remarks. The family described is not content merely to deny what is happening. Part of that denial is embodied in their desire for him to "keep quiet and undergo a treatment." Treatments then function, in part, as methods of denying death. As Illich (1976) has argued, this motive, the denial of death, has made dying or even becoming ill more distressing than it might ordinarily be because of the useless or ineffective treatments to which we are likely to

be subjected. One of the illustrations he has used is the tonsillec-
tomy, where the rate of unnecessary surgery is enormous.

DISCUSSION: CLINICAL EPISTEMOLOGY

Depression, paranoia, dying, and, perhaps, other conditions
not discussed strike in some way at the fabric of our society.
These considerations open up a new field that might be called
"clinical epistemology." Epistemology is the study of how we
acquire our knowledge. The paranoid appears to acquire his
knowledge of right and wrong, real and unreal differently from
the majority. Perhaps as a result of the shock of loss, the depressive also seems to see things differently from those around him,
or inadvertently forces upon them insights that they do not
desire. The dying patient is another outsider; he might expose
the futility of our medical procedures and the inevitability of our
own deaths.

One can argue, and it is easy to be sympathetic to this point
of view, that the strategy of choice is to redevelop the self-decep-
tion and social membership that accompanies it in those psychiatric situations in which it is required. Goffman (1952) referred
to this function of psychotherapy critically as "cooling the mark
out." He compared it to the necessity for con men to make sure
that the mark, or victim, did not protest and make trouble about
being conned. The physician in Ibsen's *The Wild Duck* encourages the perpetuation of family or individual hypocrisy, which
he cynically refers to as the "vital lie":

RELLING: Most of the world is sick, I'm afraid.
GREGERS: And what's your prescription for Hjalmar?
RELLING: My standard one. I try to keep the vital lie in him. . . .
           Deprive the average man of his vital lie, and you've
           robbed him of happiness as well.

It is also possible to adopt a reformist strategy. There are dis-
senters who believe that the all-too-common approach of keeping alive the vital lie leaves a society surrounded by a thick wall
of lethargy, "covered over with layers of dead skin, accumula-

tions of habit, spontaneity buried under years of mechanical gestures. The living center is almost choked by debris and—what is worse—man has come to be content with living in the midst of this offal" (Ostrovsky 1967, p.11). Under such conditions radical and typically painful intervention is indicated to bring about change, to clear away this psychological pollution. Adoption of this strategy leads to a radical psychotherapy which may entail the opening by the therapist of a Pandora's box containing all the inhuman things that humans do to each other, to the extent of questioning the very fragile nature of our social fabric, our social ecology. This strategy somewhat parallels developments in the Theatre of the Absurd, which espouses the idea that the public must be unsettled, irritated, overpowered, and forced to react violently in order to react authentically and not hypocritically. Those who recommend it point out that at the very bottom of Pandora's box Zeus took pity and placed Hope.

This sort of epistemological intervention, like genetic engineering, is fraught with dangers which can hardly be foreseen. How to proceed and along what path, what strategy to take, is for the future to decide.

Epilogue

THE ENDGAME

It is never any good dwelling on goodbyes.
It is not the being together that it prolongs,
it is the parting.

Elizabeth Asquith Bibesco
The Fir and the Palm, 1924

CHAPTER 9

Exiting

TERMINATION of psychotherapy has always been considered in different terms from its counterpart in other professional relationships. It is easy to understand why a seven-year experience of trice-weekly sessions that has had as its goal the total reconstruction of the personality requires such special consideration. In contrast, strategic psychotherapy can adopt the model of briefer and more limited professional relationships.

Under the best of conditions, relationships with professionals other than psychotherapists are not regarded as terminating at all. They are seen as intermittent. For example, the accountant, lawyer, family doctor, or barber may have permanent relationships with clients and perhaps their families, although the actual face-to-face contacts occur only for specific tasks or problems. Particularly in relationships of confidence, as in the case of the accountant and the physician, the tie may last a lifetime. The brevity of the actual contact and less ambitious goals, in contrast with those of psychoanalysis, make the task of exiting a relatively easy event.

THERAPEUTIC GOALS

It is frequently helpful if the therapist keeps in mind the distinction between a life goal and a therapy goal. Achievement of life goals is not an appropriate criterion for ending therapy. For example, a woman approaching the age of thirty may wish to get married and enters therapy because she is depressed about her chances. In this case marriage is a life goal, and the amount of assistance a therapist can render toward achieving this end is limited. He may, on the other hand, be able to help the patient deal with the decreasing probability of marriage in some other fashion.

In addition to the distinction between life and therapy goals, it is also helpful to draw the distinction between two types of therapy goals: cure (or total mental health) and the more realistic goal of amelioration. When a physician takes an eyelash out of someone's eye, or corrects a minor dislocated but not fractured bone, the event resembles the public's concept of "cure." The patient blinks his eye or wiggles his toe, smiles broadly, and says, "It's gone. I'm cured." However, as a model of therapy— whether medical, surgical, or psychiatric—these procedures are quite misleading. From a contrasting point of view, therapists are assumed to influence the natural healing and recuperative power of the patient. "I bandage; nature cures" is the old medical adage. Often the goal of any therapy is to make it possible for the patient to live with his disease. For some reason it is frequently the pschiatrist who is criticized for not being able to cure his patients completely, while the cardiologist, for example, is judged by less rigorous standards.

In strategic psychotherapy the therapist should be prepared to "fade" himself out of the picture at one of two points: when progress toward a solution has begun, and when it is reasonably clear that progress is not likely to occur. At the point where the patient can more or less see the light at the end of the tunnel, when he appears to be on the right track, recognizes that he is making progress, understands the tasks before him, and has his spirits lifted sufficiently to complete them enthusiastically, the therapist is obviously less necessary. He can schedule appointments with the patient that are at greater intervals and of shorter duration. Simultaneously, care must be taken to demonstrate continuing concern. However, a telephone call initiated by the therapist that lasts five minutes probably demonstrates this better than a scheduled session. Careful initial briefing will also prevent a misinterpretation of quickly decreased sessions.

At the earliest possible moment in therapy, preferably in the first session, this general concept of exiting should be transmitted to the patient; the distinction between life and therapy goals and, if possible, between total health and the increasing cost-benefit ratio should be explained. It is important to consider whether to disabuse any patient of the goal of miraculous, unrealistic cure, yet at the same time point out to him that a short series of sessions is all that is necessary to get the ball rolling. For example, a patient with a phobia will probably be required to deal with some anxiety for several years. It is unlikely to disappear completely, like the discomfort in one's eye when a cinder is removed. Although considerable relief might be found in a short series of sessions, the patient might find it necessary to continue to cope with the problem on his own for a while, with only the briefest of contacts with the therapist. Whether or not he considers himself "cured," and at what point in time, will be discussed below.

The door can always be left open for the patient to return to discuss other aspects of the presenting problem. If exiting has occurred before the estimated or expected number of sessions offered in the initial interview, it is sometimes said that the patient has the remaining few sessions "in the bank."

By the therapist's not insisting on a rigid termination, it is unlikely that the patient will react with negativism and attempt to demand further sessions. Therapists frequently forget that psychotherapy of any variety is usually judged to be an aversive experience. It costs money, is at inconvenient times, and deals on some level with personal failure. It is, as I have already mentioned, an ordeal. This has two important consequences. First, most patients will gladly terminate at the earliest moment. Second, if prolonged it can act as a punishment for improvement. The patient can improve in the first weeks of therapy. The therapist can choose to ignore this or belittle it by labeling it a "flight into health," and throw the weight of his authority behind the decision to continue therapy. The patient relapses as the therapist has "predicted," and therapy is thereby prolonged considerably.

In "time-limited therapy" (Mann 1973), in which a rigid termination is upheld and strongly emphasized (for example, by emphatically making note of the last session in an appointment book in front of the patient), it is possible to provoke a reaction from almost all patients. The reaction can then be studied much like transference is studied in psychoanalysis. There is also the possibility that a substitution will occur in which concern about termination of therapy, usually in twelve sessions, will take the place of the presenting complaint. The success with which time-limited therapy has been able to provoke reactions to termination suggests that some care should be given to obtaining consensual agreement about the goals of psychotherapy and termination in order to prevent an unwanted reaction.

The conduct of the therapy session itself can transmit certain expectations to the patient. If there is an agenda, there is simultaneously an unexpressed expectation of termination at its end. On the other hand, if the session begins with "talk about whatever you want" or "start wherever you like" (and this occurs at the beginning of every session), there is the implication of timelessness which ultimately finds its expression in years rather than months of therapy.

One of the most effective ways to lay the groundwork for termination is in the handling of appointments. Rather than sign a patient up for a particular hour each week, as for an academic course, the next appointment can be determined at the end of each session. It can be made for the next day or in two weeks, depending upon many factors. Rather than say, "We'll be meeting Tuesday at 9 o'clock (from now on)" the therapist can take out his appointment book, think about the appropriate time, and vary it based on the patient's or his own schedule. In this way a limited duration is suggested to the patient.

UNSUCCESSFUL CASES

Surgeons, it is said, bury their failures, architects plant ivy, and lawyers visit them in prison, but the psychotherapist's unsuccessful cases return, frequently weekly. If one allows this state of affairs to prevail, if one's unsuccessful cases remain in therapy interminably while successful ones are quickly discharged, in a very short time one's caseload will become more and more inflexible, filled up with permanent, unsuccessful patients. Many of these patients are using the psychotherapy experience as a socializing event. For example, a very overweight woman continued to visit me although she did not lose a pound. I discovered that she was so lonely that she would call the telephone operator to hear a human voice. Her weekly sessions with me were only officially about weight loss. I had become "a friend." The purchase of friendship, although common in psychotherapy, does not seem to me to be an efficient use of funds or professional time. In this case, plans to find an alternative solution were put into effect with considerable success. (I suggested she attend a community group at which she was able to make friends.)

I do not mean to suggest that several approaches to a problem might not be tried, or that the therapist should not attempt to look for new factors or conceptualizations of the problem presented by the patient. In fact, it is helpful to suggest to the patient at the outset that there are several possible strategies toward a problem, and that if one doesn't work another might be tried. However, there may come a point when it is clear that the therapy will not work. The patient should then be told that the cost of continuing outweighs the cost of terminating. For example, I saw a young woman for weight loss who had tried many different therapies. Each time she had entered therapy, she gained weight; when she was not in therapy she managed to lose. I pointed this out to her and suggested that the attention given to the problem seemed to make it worse. We terminated after five sessions.

THE SOCIOLOGICAL PERSPECTIVE

From a sociological rather than psychiatric perspective, there are four role outcomes for the patient in psychotherapy: dropout, permanent patient, permanent nonpatient, and therapist.

A dropout is someone who enters therapy and in a short time initiates termination, with or without benefit. In brief psychotherapy "dropping out" can be the ideal outcome, assuming specified goals have been attained. It has been observed that, if a patient attends more than approximately ten sessions, he is likely to continue for several years, and psychotherapy becomes part of his life. In certain clinical situations an effort is made to "make a patient" out of the person coming for help, and supervision often is offered novice therapists on how to accomplish this transformation of identity and expectations. The result may be the sociological status of permanent patient.

Certain sociological investigators consider such a process a "degradation ceremony" (Garfinkel 1956). From this point of view, dropout status might be preferable since, as with other stigmatizing labels that are ostensibly assigned for the subject's benefit, there is virtually no way to shed the identity of mental patient. It has been demonstrated (Tringo 1970) that the public is less tolerant of mental patients or ex-mental patients than any other disabled group, including ex-convicts and alcoholics. It may thus be at best a mixed blessing to induct a person with problems into the long-term patient role.

A permanent nonpatient is someone who has had considerable therapy which has been terminated. However, he then joins a group of ex-patients or cult members with whom he spends most of his time. For example, after undergoing one of the more esoteric treatment experiences, such as primal scream therapy, the former patient may prefer to remain with others like himself. The result may be a cult surrounding the originator of the therapy. Many therapies share these characteristics in more subtle form, with varying degrees of confinement within the cult.

A variation of this pattern has appeared recently on the American scene in the form of semireligious cults, often with a mystic or Eastern philosophical orientation, which attract those who cannot or perhaps do not choose to function in conventional social roles. Members of such cults are not necessarily drawn from the ranks of former patients, but otherwise they resemble the permanent nonpatient described here. There is some controversy among professionals about whether membership in a cult, particularly one that demands total commitment, serves the same function for certain vulnerable adolescents and adults, with perhaps less stigma, as psychiatric hospitalization. This must be determined empirically, but it illustrates that permanent patient or permanent nonpatient status (cult member) might be a useful experience for certain people at certain periods in their lives.

One of the most successful outcomes of lengthy psychotherapy is "therapist." Years ago I saw a couple prior to their divorce. More recently I met the ex-wife on the street and asked her what she had been doing. She rattled off the most remarkable list of therapies which she had undergone. I half-facetiously suggested that she now knew more than most people about the field and, perhaps, should consider becoming a therapist—if only to cash in on her investment. About two years later I received an announcement in the mail that she had entered practice. She had attended an institute for laymen and had successfully combined her former artistic career with therapy.

Many of those who are in long-term therapy intend to become therapists themselves—much more than is generally appreciated. I lectured at one well-known graduate school and made the aforementioned statement. The chairman of the department, who knew all of his postgraduate students and all of the training analysts, did some calculations based on which student was in training analysis with which supervisor and concluded that the senior analysts did not have time to see anyone who was not planning to become an analyst.

In summary, from a sociological perspective, therapeutic goals might suitably embrace any of the four outcomes. Cults attempt to create permanent nonpatients; other therapies attempt to create permanent patients. The goal of brief therapy is the satisfied dropout. The goal of training analysis is therapist.

BREAKING THE SPELL OF ILLNESS

Although some patients recognize independently that therapy termination is impending, many others are unable or unwilling to make this judgment on their own. Regular therapy sessions can acquire the comforting characteristics of a ritual, a crutch, a structural framework around which to plan one's daily activities, especially for nonworking women who are customarily overrepresented in private practice. The role of patient also becomes comfortable and reassuring, entailing as it often does the transfer of responsibility and often decision-making powers to an "expert" who becomes the agent of change. In addition to its supportive qualities, sustained therapy provides the patient with evidence that he is trying to do something about his problems, and that someone is available, willing, and able to help. These factors together tend to encourage continuation of therapy, and make the prospect of termination somewhat worrisome to many patients, even if they have accomplished a great deal in treatment. Patients with an external locus of control are particularly reluctant to terminate therapy, lacking as they do any faith in their own powers of control and mastery.

Termination is most effectively and easily brought about if its occurrence has been anticipated from the very first stage of treatment. Nevertheless, the patient must at some point conclude independently that his problem is solved, that he is no longer ill, or that relief has been achieved. Like the issue of morale, this is essentially an attitudinal component or outlook, amenable to therapeutic influence.

In chapter 1 it was pointed out that people do not "get sick," that illness is a state of mind, often a decision made in consultation with someone in the medical profession. The same considerations apply to cure. One can argue that illness occurs when a decision is made to that effect, and so it always entails an abrupt change of mental set. Therefore, "not being ill" or "cure" also occurs suddenly (when we use the term to refer to the sudden change in set that follows the decision). In both the illness and the cure process the actual bodily phenomena are not always the major determinant of the decision. One can remain physiologically ill but think of oneself as "cured." The reverse is also possible. Day (1962) vividly describes the necessity of using particular techniques to influence favorably this decision-making process. After discussing the unintentional influence that doctors sometimes exert on patients to keep them invalids, he presents his technique of the "therapeutic physical exam," during which he tells the patient what is right and healthy with him: "Your kidneys are behaving like perfect little gentlemen . . . that's a good strong heart you've got there. . . . Your low E.S.R. rules out the possibility of any progressive active disease process anywhere . . ." (Day 1962, p. 213).

Gillis (1974) has also noted that at the end of psychotherapy it is necessary for the patient to come to the conclusion that he is now cured. Gillis goes so far as to suggest that the therapist may want to argue as strongly as he can that the patient is now totally recovered. There are times, of course, when the patient arrives at this conclusion without assistance. However, some attention must be paid to this issue in every treatment situation. A patient with a more internal locus of control will be better able to accept the notion that there is no such thing as a "cure," but that one gradually improves over a period of time in relation to the amount of work one puts in. Patients with more external loci of control will not be able to accept this sort of notion of improvement. Although one may attempt to get them to perform the same tasks, the context in which the tasks must be put has to include the concept of a discontinuous moment when they are cured.

In many forms of therapeutic intervention, the patient and perhaps his family rely on the authority in charge for a cue that the treatment was effective. A trivial incident when I was a medical student illustrated this transactional nature of "cure." At the time I lived in an apartment below a lower-class family. One day the parents rang my doorbell very upset because their youngest child, an infant, had cut himself on a razor blade. I raced upstairs thinking that a real disaster had occurred (and wondering how I was going to deal with it). When I arrived I found that the child had a small laceration on his finger. I ran downstairs again, got a small Band-Aid, returned, and placed it over the cut. Looking up after my ministrations, I saw that the family was just as anxious as before. "Well," I said, "that emergency is over." Everyone sighed, their stiff postures relaxed, small talk was exchanged in a somewhat festive mood, and I went back to my studies thoroughly puzzled by what had happened.

More recently I was asked to see a patient who had been "possessed." In a mixture of metaphors she was admitted to a psychiatric hospital and cured by psychopharmacology. However, she still believed that she was suffering from her original complaints. It was not that she was actually doing or feeling any of the distressing things that she had done or felt before, but that her opinion of what had been done for her failed to lead to the conclusion that she was no longer possessed. What was necessary in this case were certain moves that would enable her to conclude that she was indeed cured. With this particular patient all that was necessary was to make the authoritative statement that an expert on possession had seen her and declared her no longer in danger.

One of the usual procedures of witch doctors is to remove the offending agent from the patient. In most cases some sleight of hand is required to appear to take out of a patient a bloody piece of cotton or some other easily palmed object. Occasionally the witch doctor sucks the offending agent out, and this allows him to hide it in his mouth. By so doing he is clearly and distinctly forcing on the patient the conclusion that he is now "cured." Levi-Strauss (1963) describes the puzzlement of a young apprentice witch doctor when he realizes that the hoax works. That is, his patients get better when he does nothing but pretend to remove the offending agent. He is even further puzzled to find that the procedure works even if he has exposed other witch doctors for doing the same thing. This is similar to Frank's (1973) study in which placebos were successfully given to patients who have been told that they were going to receive placebos.

In the patient with an external locus of control it is necessary, borrowing Day's terminology, to break the spell of illness. This can be achieved by creating an arbitrary endpoint. For example, it can be determined that when the patient can allow a dog to lick him, his phobia is over. At other times a psychological test might be used to determine that the patient is now cured. Care must be taken to make sure that the patient does not determine that some hypothetical offending agent (such as a job or his wife) must be removed in order for him to feel better. For example, a physician came to see me who many years before had had a severe anxiety attack and had then, on his own, determined that he would feel better if his wife were not with him .He precipitously divorced her, left his three children, and had been suffering legally, financially, and psychologically since that time. What is worse, his anxiety attacks did not end.

Other techniques that sometimes facilitate the termination of illness include the authoritative statement by the therapist that the illness is over, or referral back to the original source for this physician to make the statement. It must be remembered that when more than one person has been involved in the decision that someone is ill, it is necessary to involve the others in the decision that the patient is now better. This can apply to the family, school, or family doctor. On occasion a ceremony for an entire family to perform can be helpful. This can entail a celebration, such as going out to dinner.

Hypnotists sometimes suggest a "double-take" ending to a problem. The patient is told that at some time he will suddenly realize that he has been functioning perfectly well for an extended period. For example, he will find himself in elevators without his usual phobic reaction. This avoids creating negativism by insisting that the patient is cured, licenses forgetting about a problem (which in itself can be therapeutic), and takes into account that the decision "I am cured" is relatively independent of actual behavior.

In the final session, after a review, I try to turn the topic back to general small talk, somewhat like the casual conversation that occurred in the waiting room before therapy began. I make an effort to return to a symmetrical or equal relationship with the patient. Questions might be asked by me or by the patient that have nothing to do with therapy. If the patient's hobby is camping, I might ask a few questions about it, or the patient might find the occasion to ask me about something that he has noticed —my dog, for example, who is frequently in the office with me. At a certain point there is a cadence, a point at which the rhythm of this sort of talk comes to a stop for a moment or two. At this point it is time to say goodbye.

At the door I shake the patient's hand and wish him luck.

APPENDIXES
REFERENCES
INDEX

APPENDIX A

Outline of

Initial Interview

I. *Pinpointing the Problem*
    a. the complaint
    b. intense emotional reaction

II. *What Is the Patient's (Family's) Own Strategy Toward This Problem?*

III. *What Is the Patient's (Family's) Own Expectation of Therapy?*
    a. the consumer approach
    b. debriefing regarding other therapeutic experiences
    c. briefing regarding this therapy
        frequency of visits
        criterion of termination
        homework
        fees, etc.

IV. *What Change in the Patient's (Family's) Strategy Do You Think Would Be Helpful?*

V. *The Diagnosis*
    a. the name
    b. the explanation (brief)
    c. confidence in cure, power of methods, success with similar cases
    d. HOWEVER, depends upon
        i. hard work
        ii. there being no secrets

VI.   *Preparation for a Direct Request for Change in Strategy*
      a.   admissions
            of failure
            of seriousness
            of reality of the problem
            of urgency for solution
      b.   mobilization of hope
            limiting move
            ripple effect
            ordeals (pilgrimages, obstacles)
            prestige work
            belief in self, enthusiasm
            interest shown in patient
                  warm, flattering remarks
                  No-miss, Aunt Fanny interpretations
            intense emotional reaction
                  Primal Scream techniques
                  Imagery techniques
                  attribution work

VII.   *Preparation for an Indirect Request for Change in Strategy*
      a.   positive connotation, utilization techniques
      b.   suggestions delivered as asides
      c.   confusion techniques
      d.   licenses
      e.   flattery

APPENDIX B

Protocol

for Age Regression

Now concentrate carefully upon what I have to say. I am going to suggest that you go back in time, back into the past. You will feel as if you were back in the period I suggest. Let us start with yesterday. What did you do yesterday morning? What did you have for breakfast? For lunch? Now we are going back to the first day you came to see me. Can you see yourself talking to me? How did you feel? Describe it. What clothes did you wear? Now listen carefully. We are going back to a period when you were little. You are getting smaller. You are getting smaller and smaller. Your arms and legs are getting smaller. I am someone you know and like. You are between ten and twelve. Can you see yourself? Describe what you see. Now you are getting even smaller. You are becoming very, very little. Your arms and legs are shrinking. Your body is shrinking. You are going back to a time when you were very, very little. Now you are entering school for the first time. Can you see yourself? Who is your teacher? How old are you? What are your friends' names? Now you are even smaller than that; you are very, very much smaller. Your mother is holding you. Do you see yourself with mother? What is she wearing? What is she saying?

Wolberg, 1945

APPENDIX C

Hypnotic Induction
Procedure and Scale
Based on Sleep Model

PHASE ONE (SKIP TO PARAGRAPH 8 WHEN SUBJECT'S
EYES CLOSE)

1. Keep your eyes on that little light and listen carefully to what I say. Your ability to be hypnotized depends entirely on your willingness to cooperate. It has nothing to do with your intelligence. As for your willpower—if you want, you can remain awake all the time and pay no attention to me. In that case you might make me look silly, but you are only wasting time. On the other hand, if you pay close attention to what I say, and follow what I tell you, you can easily learn to fall into hypnotic sleep. In that case you will be helping this experiment and not wasting any time. Hypnosis is nothing fearful or mysterious. It is merely a state of strong interest in some particular thing. In a sense you are hypnotized whenever you see a good show and forget you are part of the audience, but instead feel you are part of the story. Your cooperation, your interest is what I ask of you. Your ability to be hypnotized is a measure of your willingness to cooperate. Nothing will be done that will in any way cause you the least embarrassment.

2. Now relax and make yourself entirely comfortable. Keep your eyes on that little light. Keep staring at it all the time. Keep staring as hard as you can, as long as you can.

3. Relax completely. Relax every muscle of your body. Relax the muscles of your leg. Relax the muscles of your arms. Make yourself perfectly comfortable. Let yourself be limp, limp, limp. Relax more and more, more and more. Relax completely. Relax completely. Relax completely.

4. Your legs feel heavy and limp, heavy and limp. Your arms are heavy, heavy, heavy, heavy as lead. Your whole body feels heavy, heavier and heavier. You feel tired and sleepy, tired and sleepy. You feel drowsy and sleepy, drowsy and sleepy. Your breathing is slow and regular, slow and regular.

5. Your eyes are tired from staring. Your eyes are wet from straining. The strain in your eyes is getting greater and greater, greater and greater. You would like to close your eyes and relax completely, relax completely (but keep your eyes open just a little longer, just a little longer.) You will soon reach your limit. The strain will be so great, your eyes will be so tired, your lids will become so heavy, your eyes will close of themselves, close of themselves.

6. And then you will be completely relaxed, completely relaxed. Warm and comfortable, warm and comfortable. Tired and drowsy. Tired and sleepy. Sleepy. Sleepy. Sleepy. You are paying attention to nothing but the sound of my voice. You hear nothing but the sound of my voice.

7. Your eyes are blurred. You can hardly see, hardly see. Your eyes are wet and uncomfortable. Your eyes are strained. The strain is getting greater, greater and greater, greater and greater. Your lids are heavy. Heavy as lead. Getting heavier and heavier, heavier and heavier. They're pushing down, down, down. Your lids seem weighted, weighted with lead, heavy as lead, your eyes are blinking, blinking, closing, closing.

8. You feel drowsy and sleepy, drowsy and sleepy. I shall now begin counting. At each count you will feel yourself going down, down, down into a deep comfortable, a deep restful sleep. Listen carefully. One–down, down, down. Two–three–four–more and more, more and more. Five–six–seven–eight–you are sinking, sinking. Nine–ten–eleven–twelve–deeper and deeper, deeper and deeper. Thirteen–fourteen–fifteen–sixteen–(If eyes close): You are falling fast asleep. (If open): Your eyes are closing, closing. Seventeen–eighteen–nineteen–twenty–(If closed): You are sound asleep, fast asleep. (If open): Begin at paragraph 2 and repeat.

PERIOD IN WHICH EYES CLOSED	SCORE VALUE
1	5
2	4
3	3
4	2
5	1
Eyes do not close	0

Friedlander and Sarbin, 1938

PHASE TWO (CHALLENGES)

1. Your eyes are tightly shut, tightly shut. Your lids are glued together, glued together, tightly shut. No matter how hard you try, you cannot open your eyes, you cannot open your eyes. Try to open your eyes. Try hard as you can (pause ten seconds). Now relax completely, relax completely.

2. Your left arm is heavy, heavy as lead. Your arm is heavy as lead. You cannot raise your arm. Try hard as you can, hard as you can. You cannot bend your arm. Try hard as you can, hard as you can (pause ten seconds). Now relax completely.

3. Extend your arm, straight out, straight out. Your arm is rigid. Rigid and stiff. Stiff as a board. No matter how hard you try, you cannot bend your right arm. Try to bend your arm. Try hard as you can, hard as you can (pause ten seconds). Now relax completely, completely.

4. Put your fingers together. Interlock your fingers. Your fingers are interlocked, tightly interlocked. You cannot separate your fingers. Try hard as you can (pause ten seconds). Now relax completely, relax completely.

5. You cannot say your name. No matter how hard you try, you cannot say your name. Try to say your name. Try as hard as you can (pause ten seconds).

6. Now relax completely. I am going to wake you up. When you awake, you will remember nothing of what has happened, nothing of what has happened. I shall count to ten. At eight you will open your eyes. At ten you will be wide awake and feeling cheerful. But you will remember nothing of what has happened. After you awake, you will hear someone calling your name. Ready, now, one, two, etc. . . . .

7. (When the subject awakens, wait ten seconds. If no response, ask: "Do you hear anything?" If the reply is "Yes," ask, "What?" If "No," ask, "Did you hear your name being called?")

CRITERION	SCORE VALUE
Number of suggestions passed	
5	5
4	4
3	3
2	2
1	1
0	0

Friedlander and Sarbin, 1938

APPENDIX D

Protocol for

Covert Sensitization

I want you to imagine. . . . As you are about to . . . you get a funny feeling in the pit of your stomach. You start to feel queasy, nauseous and sick all over. As you . . . you can feel food particles inching up your throat. You're just about to vomit. As you . . . the food comes up into your mouth. You try to keep your mouth closed because you are afraid that you'll spit up the . . . all over the place. You continue to . . . by. . . . As you're about to . . . you puke; you vomit all over your hands, the . . . and the. . . . It goes all over the . . . over other people's clothes, food, etc. Your eyes are watering. Snot and mucus are all over your mouth and nose. Your hands feel sticky. There is an awful smell. As you look at this mess you just can't help but vomit again and again until just watery stuff is coming out. Everyone is looking at you with shocked expressions. You turn away from the . . . and immediately start to feel better. You run out of the room, and as you run out, you feel better and better and better. You wash and clean yourself up, and it feels wonderful.

You have just. . . . As soon as you make that decision, you start to get that funny feeling in the pit of your stomach. You say, "Oh, oh; Oh No; I won't. . . ." Then you immediately feel calm and comfortable.

Cautela, 1967

APPENDIX E

Protocol for

Negative Practice

Usually we consider that practicing an act makes it easier for us to perform that act. That is often the case, but sometimes where we have learned an act, as you seem to have learned your stutter (or whatever behavioral symptom the patient presents), we find that in order to get rid of the act we have to repeat it, i.e., practice it. This may sound paradoxical, but by repetition, by practice, we hope to bring your "involuntary" response back under "voluntary" control—which means that you regain control over the response. The procedure for doing this involves your close cooperation. When you come for your practice sessions, we shall sit and chat—about anything you like—and during your conversation, I shall stop you and ask you to reproduce the act you wish to eliminate. The attempt to reproduce the act will be difficult at first . . . but I'll try to help you in many different ways to do it correctly. Your job is to try to follow the instructions and to remember that you are practicing a response which you wish to eliminate.

Lehner, 1954

REFERENCES

Aldrich, C. K. 1968. Brief psychotherapy: A reappraisal of some theoretical assumptions. *American Journal of Psychotherapy* 125:585–592.

Auerswald, E. A. 1971. Families, change, and the ecological perspective. *Family Process* 10:263–280.

Ayllon, T. 1965. Intensive treatment of psychotic behavior by stimulus satiation and food reinforcement. In *Case studies in behavior modification,* ed. L. Ullman and L. Krasner. New York: Holt, Rinehart.

Bakan, P. 1969. Hypnotizability, laterality of eye movements and functional brain asymmetry. *Perceptual and Motor Skills* 28: 927–932.

Balint, M. 1957. *The doctor, the patient and his illness.* New York: International Universities Press.

Barber, T. X. 1969. Review of *Advanced techniques of hypnosis and therapy: Selected papers of Milton Erickson, M.D.,* ed. J. Haley. *Psychiatry* 32:221–225.

Barber, T. X., and Calverley, D. S. 1964. Toward a theory of hypnotic behavior: Effects of suggestibility of defining the situation as hypnosis and defining response to suggestion as easy. *Journal of Abnormal and Social Psychology* 68:585–592.

Bateson, G.; Jackson, D.; Haley, J.; and Weakland, J. 1956. Towards a theory of schizophrenia. *Behavioral Science* 1:251–264.

Baudouin, C. 1920. *Suggestion and autosuggestion.* London: Allen & Unwin.

Benedeck, T. 1937. Defense mechanisms and structure of the total personality. *Psychoanalytic Quarterly* 6:96–118.

Benson, H.; Beary, J.; and Carol, M. 1974. The relaxation response. *Psychiatry* 37:37–45.

Bowen, M. 1966. The use of family theory in clinical practice. *Comprehensive Psychiatry* 7:345–373.

Boyd, J. R.; Covington, T. R.; Stanaszek, W. F.; and Coussons, J. 1974. Drug defaulting, part 1: Determinants of compliance. *American Journal of Hospital Pharmacology* 31:362–367.

Breuer, J., and Freud, S. 1895. Studies on hysteria. In *The standard edition of the complete psychological works of Sigmund Freud*, trans. James Strachey (London: Hogarth, 1955) 2:3–305.

Bruch, H. 1974. Perils of behavior modification in treatment of anorexia nervosa. *Journal of the American Medical Association* 230:1419–1422.

————. 1975. Point of view. *Frontiers of Psychiatry* 5:1–8.

Cautela, J. R. 1967. Covert sensitization. *Psychological Reports* 20:459–468.

Cohen, M. B.; Baker, G.; Cohen, R. A.; Fromm-Reichmann, F.; and Weigert, E. V. 1954. An intensive study of twelve cases of manic-depressive psychosis. *Psychiatry* 17:103–137.

Cooper, L. M. 1966. Spontaneous and suggested posthypnotic source amnesia. *International Journal of Clinical and Experimental Hypnosis* 14:180–193.

Coyne, J. C. 1976. Toward an interactional description of depression. *Psychiatry* 39:29–40.

Day, G. 1962. Spellbinding and spellbreaking in convalescence. *Lancet* January 27:211–213.

Denniston, D., and McWilliams, P. 1975. *The TM book: How to enjoy the rest of your life*. Allen Park, Mich.: Versemonger.

Diamond, M. J. 1974. Modification of hypnotizability: A review. *Psychological Bulletin* 81:180–198.

Dollard, J., and Miller, N. E. 1950. *Personality and psychotherapy*. New York: McGraw-Hill.

Dunlap, K. 1928. A revision of the fundamental law of habit formation. *Science* 67:360–362.

Eissler, R. S. 1949. Scapegoats of society. In *Searchlights on delinquency*, ed. K. R. Eissler. New York: International Universities Press.

Ellenberger, H. F. 1966. The pathogenic secret and its therapeutics. *Journal of the History of the Behavioral Sciences* 2:29–42.

————. 1970. *The discovery of the unconscious*. New York: Basic Books.

Ellis, A. 1962. *Reason and emotion in psychotherapy*. New York: Lyle Stuart.

Erickson, M. 1952. Deep hypnosis and its induction. In *Experimental hypnosis,* ed. L. M. LeCron. New York: Macmillan. (Also in Haley 1967)

———. 1959. Further techniques of hypnosis—utilization techniques. *American Journal of Clinical Hypnosis* 2:3–21. (Also in Haley 1967.)

———. 1962. The identification of a secure reality. *Family Process* 1:294–303. (Also in Haley 1967)

———. 1964a. Pantomime techniques in hypnosis and the implications. *American Journal of Clinical Hypnosis* 7:64–70.

———. 1964b. The confusion technique in hypnosis. *American Journal of Clinical Hypnosis* 6:183–207. (Also in Haley 1967)

Eysenck, H. J. 1957. *Sense and nonsense in psychology.* Baltimore: Penguin.

Frank, J. 1973. *Persuasion and healing: A comparative study of psychotherapy.* Baltimore: Johns Hopkins University Press.

Frankl, V. 1960. Paradoxical intention: A logotherapeutic technique. *American Journal of Psychotherapy* 14:520–535.

Freud, A. 1946. *The ego and mechanisms of defense.* New York: International Universities Press.

Freud, S. 1918. From the history of an infantile neurosis. In *The standard edition of the complete psychological works of Sigmund Freud,* trans. James Strachey (London: Hogarth, 1955) 17:7–122.

Friedlander, J. W., and Sarbin, T. R. 1938. The depth of hypnosis. *Journal of Abnormal and Social Psychology* 33:281–294.

Fromm-Reichmann, F. 1959. *Psychoanalysis and psychotherapy: Selected papers.* Chicago: University of Chicago Press.

Garfield, S. L. 1971. Research on client variables in psychotherapy. In *Handbook of psychotherapy and behavior change,* ed. A. E. Bergin and S. L. Garfield. New York: Wiley.

Garfinkel, H. 1956. Conditions of successful degradation ceremonies. *American Journal of Sociology* 61:420–424.

Gill, M. M., and Brenman, M. 1959. *Hypnosis and related states.* New York: International Universities Press.

Gillis, J. S. 1974. Social influence therapy: The therapist as manipulator. *Psychology Today* December:91–95.

Goffman, E. 1952. On cooling the mark out: Some aspects of adaptation to failure. *Psychiatry* 15:451–463.

———. 1961. *Asylums: Essays on the social situation of mental patients and other inmates.* Chicago: Aldine.

Gurin, G.; Veroff, J.; and Feld, S. 1960. *Americans view their mental health: A nation-wide interview survey.* Joint Commission of Mental Illness and Health Monograph Series 4. New York: Basic Books.

Haley, J. 1963. *Strategies of psychotherapy.* New York: Grune & Stratton.

————, ed. 1967. *Advanced techniques of hypnosis and therapy: Selected papers of M. H. Erickson, M.D.* New York: Grune & Stratton.

————. 1973a. *Uncommon therapy: The psychiatric techniques of Milton H. Erickson, M.D.* New York: Norton.

————. 1973b. Strategic therapy when a child is presented as the problem. *Journal of the American Academy of Child Psychiatry* 12:641–659.

Hammer, M. 1967. The directed daydream technique. *Psychotherapy: Theory, Research and Practice* 4:173–181.

Hansell, N. 1976. *The person-in-distress: On the biosocial dynamics of adaptation.* New York: Behavioral Publications.

Hare-Mustin, R. T. 1975. Treatment of temper tantrums by a paradoxical intervention. *Family Process* 14:481–486.

Harper, R. A. 1975. *The new psychotherapies.* Englewood Cliffs, N.J.: Prentice-Hall.

Heiman, M. 1956. The relationship between man and dog. *Psychoanalytic Quarterly* 25:568–585.

Hess, W. R. 1957. *Functional organization of the diencephalon.* New York: Grune & Stratton.

Hilgard, E. R. 1975. Hypnosis. *Annual Review of Psychology* 26: 19–44.

Hilgard, E. R., and Cooper, L. M. 1965. Spontaneous and suggested posthypnotic amnesia. *International Journal of Clinical and Experimental Hypnosis* 13:261–273.

Hilgard, E. R., and Hilgard, J. R. 1975. *Hypnosis in the relief of pain.* Los Altos, Calif.: William Kaufman.

Hilgard, J. R. 1974. Imaginative involvement: Some characteristics of the highly hypnotizable and the non-hypnotizable. *International Journal of Clinical and Experimental Hypnosis* 22:135–156.

Homme, I. E. 1965. Perspectives in psychology. XXIV: Control of coverants, the operants of the mind. *Psychological Record* 15: 501–511.

Hubert, H. P., and Mauss, M. 1953. Interpretation of the sacrificial ceremony. In *Primitive heritage,* ed. M. Mead and N. Calas. New York: Random House.

Ibsen, H. 1965. *The wild duck.* In *Four major plays,* vol. 1. New York: Signet Classics.

Illich, I. 1976. *Medical nemesis.* New York: Pantheon.

Jackson, D. 1963. A suggestion for the technical handling of paranoid patients. *Psychiatry* 26:306–307.

———. 1968. The question of family homeostasis. In *Communication, family and marriage,* ed. D. Jackson. Palo Alto, Calif.: Science and Behavior Books.

Jacobson, E. 1938. *Progressive relaxation.* Chicago: University of Chicago Press.

———. 1954. Transference problems in the psychoanalytic treatment of severely depressed patients. *Journal of the American Psychoanalytic Association* 2:595–606.

Jacobson, N., and Martin, B. 1976. Behavioral marriage therapy: Current status. *Psychological Bulletin* 83:540–556.

Janet, P. 1925. *Psychological healing,* vol. 2. London: Allen & Unwin.

Johnson, A. M., and Szurek, S. A. 1952. The genesis of antisocial acting out in children and adults. *Psychoanalytic Quarterly* 21: 323–343.

Joint Commission on Mental Illness and Health, eds. 1961. *Action for mental health.* New York: Basic Books.

Jung, C. J. 1963. *Memories, Dreams, Reflections,* ed. Aniela Jaffe. New York: Pantheon.

Kaplan, H. S. 1974. Friction and fantasy, no-nonsense therapy for six sexual malfunctions. *Psychology Today* October:65–72.

Kendrick, D. C. 1960. The theory of "conditioned inhibition" as an explanation of negative practice effects: An experimental analysis. In *Behavior therapy and the neuroses,* ed. H. J. Eysenck. New York: Pergamon.

Kolb, L. C. 1973. *Modern clinical psychiatry.* 8th ed. Philadelphia: Saunders.

Kovel, J. 1976. *A complete guide to therapy: From psychoanalysis to behavior modification.* New York: Pantheon.

Laing, R. D. 1960. *The divided self.* London: Tavistock.

Laseque, C., and Falret, J. 1877. La folie a deux ou folie communiquee. *American Medical Psychology* 17:321.

Lazare, A.; Cohen, F.; Jacobson, A.; Williams, M.; Mignone, R.;

and Zisook, S. 1972. The walk-in patient as a "customer": A key dimension in evaluation and treatment. *American Journal of Orthopsychiatry* 42:872–883.

Lazare, A.; Eisenthal, S.; and Wasserman, L. 1975. The customer approach to patienthood. *Archives of General Psychiatry* 32: 553–558.

Lazarus, A. A. 1971. Where do behavior therapists take their troubles? *Psychological Reports* 28:349–350.

Lehner, G. 1954. Negative practice as a psychotherapeutic technique. *Journal of General Psychology* 51:69–82.

Lemert, E. M. 1962. Paranoia and the dynamics of exclusion. *Sociometry* 25:2–20.

Levi-Strauss, C. 1963. *Structural anthropology.* New York: Basic Books.

Levitt, E. E. 1966. Psychotherapy research and the expectation-reality discrepancy. *Psychotherapy: Theory, Research and Practice* 3:163–166.

Lewinsohn, P. M. 1975. The behavioral study and treatment of depression. In Hersen, M.; Eissler, R. M.; and Miller, P.M., *Progress in behavior modification,* vol. 1. San Francisco: Academic Press.

Lewis, A. 1967. Problems presented by the ambiguous word "anxiety" as used in psychopathology. *Israel Annals of Psychiatry*: 105–121.

Lewis, H. R., and Streitfeld, H. S. 1972. *Growth games.* New York: Bantam Books.

Light, D., Jr. 1975. The sociological calendar: An analytic tool for field work applied to medical and psychiatric training. *American Journal of Sociology* 80:1145–1164.

Lorion, R. P. 1974. Patient and therapist variables in the treatment of low-income patients. *Psychological Bulletin* 81:344–354.

McKinnon, R. A., and Michels, R. 1971. *The psychiatric interview in clinical practice.* Philadelphia: Saunders.

Mandell, A. 1975. Pro football fumbles the drug scandal. *Psychology Today* 9:39–47.

Mann, J. 1973. *Time-limited psychotherapy.* Cambridge, Mass.: Harvard University Press.

Marshall, J. R. 1972. The expression of feelings. *Archives of General Psychiatry* 27:786–790.

Marks, I. M. 1976. The current status of behavioral psychotherapy:

Theory and practice. *American Journal of Psychiatry* 133:253–260.

Masters, W. H., and Johnson, V. E. 1970. *Human sexual inadequacy.* Boston: Little, Brown.

Menninger, K. 1963. *The vital balance.* New York: Viking.

Minuchin, S. 1974. *Families and family therapy.* Cambridge, Mass.: Harvard University Press.

Minuchin, S.; Montalvo, B.; Guerney, B.; Rosman, B.; and Shumer, F. 1967. *Families of the slums: An exploration of their structure and treatment.* New York: Basic Books.

Montalvo, B., and Haley, J. 1973. In defense of child therapy. *Family Process* 12:227–244.

Montgomery, G. T., and Crowder, E. 1972. The symptom substitution hypothesis and the evidence. *Psychotherapy: Theory, Research and Practice* 9:98–102.

Mosher, L. 1976. Searches for the treatment of schizophrenia departing from traditional approaches. *Clinical Psychiatry News* 14:2, 15.

Newton, J. R. 1968. Considerations for the psychotherapeutic technique of symptom scheduling. *Psychotherapy: Research, Theory and Practice* 5:95–103.

Ostrovsky, E. 1967. The anatomy of cruelty: Antonin Artaud, Louis-Ferdinand Celine. *Arts and Sciences (NYU)* 2:10–13.

Palazzoli, M. S. 1974. *Self starvation: From the intrapsychic to the transpersonal approach to anorexia nervosa.* London: Chaucer.

Palazzoli, M. S., and Prata, G. Paradox and counterparadox, a new model for the therapy of the family in schizophrenic transaction. Paper presented at Fifth International Symposium on Psychotherapy of Schizophrenia, Oslo, August 14–18.

Rabkin, R. 1963. Rapid eye movements while awake. *American Journal of Psychiatry* 120:499–500.

———. 1964. Conversion hysteria as social maladaption. *Psychiatry* 27:349–363.

———. 1972. Evil as a social process: The Mai Lai massacre. In *Progress in group and family therapy,* ed. C. Sager and H. K. Singer. New York: Brunner/Mazel.

———. 1976. Criticism of the clinical use of the double bind hypothesis. In *Double bind,* ed. C. Sluzki and D. Ransom. New York: Grune & Stratton.

Ravich, R., and Wyden, B. 1974. *Predictable pairing*. New York: Wyden.

Ray, S. 1976. *I deserve love*. Milbrae, Calif.: Les Femmes.

Reed, L. S.; Myers, E. S.; and Scheidemandel, P. 1972. *Health insurance and psychiatric care: Utilization and cost*. Washington, D.C.: American Psychiatric Association.

Regush, J., and Regush, N. 1974. *PSI, the other world catalogue*. New York: Putnam.

Richardson, H. B. 1945. *Patients have families*. New York: Commonwealth Fund.

Rieff, P. 1959. *Freud: The mind of the moralist*. New York: Viking.

Rosen, R. D. 1975. Psychobabble. *New Times* October 31:43–49.

Rosenhan, D. L. 1973. On being sane in insane places. *Science* 179: 250–258.

Rotter, J. B. 1954. *Social learning and clinical psychology*. Englewood Cliffs, N.J.: Prentice-Hall.

Rubin, D. 1975. Timing of ECT correlated with thought activity. *Clinical Psychiatric News* 3:23.

Ryan, W. 1971. *Blaming the victim*. New York: Vintage.

Sager, C. J.; Gundlach, R.; and Kremer, M. 1968. The married in treatment. *Archives of General Psychiatry* 19:205–217.

Schachter, D. L. 1976. The hypnogogic state: A critical review of the literature. *Psychological Bulletin* 83:452–481.

Shapiro, A. K. 1960. A contribution to the history of the placebo effect. *Behavioral Science* 5:109–135.

Shor, R. E., and Cobb, J. C. 1968. An exploratory study of hypnotic training using the concept of plateau hypnotizability as a referent. *American Journal of Clinical Hypnosis* 10:178–197.

Shorr, J. E. 1974. *Psycho-imagination theory*. New York: Stratton Intercontinental.

Singer, J. L. 1971. Imagery and daydream techniques employed in psychotherapy: Some practical and theoretical implications. In *Current topics in clinical and community psychology*, ed. C. D. Spielberger. New York: Academic Press.

————. 1974. *Imagery and daydreaming methods in psychotherapy and behavior modification*. New York: Academic Press.

Smith, A. 1976. The benefits of boredom. *Psychology Today* 9:46–51.

Snyder, C. R., and Shenkel, R. J. 1975. The P. T. Barnum effect. *Psychology Today* 8:52–55.

Spanos, N. P. 1971. Goal directed fantasy and performance of hypnotic test suggestions. *Psychiatry* 34:86–96.

Speck, R. V. 1965. The transfer of illness phenomenon in schizophrenic families. In *Psychotherapy for the whole family,* by A. S. Friedman, I. Boszormenyi-Nagy, J. Jungreis, G. Lincoln, H. Mitchell, J. Sonne, R. Speck, and G. Spivack. New York: Springer.

Speck, R. V., and Attneave, C. 1971. Network therapy. In *Changing families,* ed. J. Haley. New York: Grune & Stratton.

Sperling, O. 1944. On appersonation. *International Journal of Psychoanalysis* 25:128–132.

Spiegel, H. 1960. Hypnosis and the psychotherapeutic process. *Comprehensive Psychiatry* 1:172–185.

———. 1970. A single treatment method to stop smoking using ancillary self-hypnosis. *International Journal of Clinical Hypnosis* 18:235–250.

———. 1972. An eye-roll test for hypnotizability. *American Journal of Clinical Hypnosis* 15:25–28.

———. 1973. Hypnotic induction profile as a quick diagnostic guide. *American Journal of Orthopsychiatry* 43:270–271.

———. 1974. The grade 5 syndrome: The highly hypnotizable person. *International Journal of Clinical and Experimental Hypnosis* 22:303–319.

Spiegel, H., and Linn, L. 1969. The "ripple effect" following adjunct hypnosis in analytic psychotherapy. *American Journal of Psychiatry* 126:53–58.

Spock, B. 1957. *Baby and child care.* New York: Pocket Books.

Spoerl, O. H. 1975. Single session psychotherapy. *Diseases of the Nervous System* 36:283–285.

Srole, L.; Langner, T. S.; Michael, S. T.; Opler, M. K.; and Rennie, T. A. 1962. *Mental health in the metropolis: The midtown Manhattan study.* New York: McGraw-Hill.

Stein, M. H. 1956. The marriage bond. *Psychoanalytic Quarterly* 25:238–259.

Stoyva, J. 1973. Biofeedback techniques and the conditions for hallucinatory activity. In *The psychophysiology of thinking,* ed. F. J. McGuigan and R. A. Schoonover. New York: Academic Press.

Sullivan, H. S. 1954. *The psychiatric interview.* New York: Norton.

———. 1956. *Clinical studies in psychiatry.* New York: Norton.

Tolstoy, L. 1960. *The death of Ivan Ilych and other stories.* New York: Signet Classics.

Tomlin, E. W. F. *Simone Weil.* New Haven: Yale University Press, 1954.

Torrey, E. F. 1973. *The mind game, witchdoctors and psychiatrists.* New York: Bantam Books.

Tringo, J. L. 1970. The hierarchy of preference toward disability groups. *Journal of Special Education* 4:295–306.

Ursano, R. J., and Dressler, D. M. 1974. Brief vs. long-term psychotherapy: Treatment decision. *Journal of Nervous and Mental Diseases* 159:164–171.

Wakeham, G. 1928. Query on "A revision of the fundamental law of habit formation." *Science* 68:135–136.

Wangh, M. 1962. The "Evocation of a proxy": A psychological maneuver, its use as a defense, its purposes and genesis. *Psychoanalytic Study of the Child* 17:451–469.

Watzlawick, P. 1976. *How real is real? Communication, disinformation and confusion.* New York: Random House.

Watzlawick, P.; Beavin, J.; and Jackson, D. 1967. *Pragmatics of human communication: A study of interactional patterns, pathologies and paradoxes.* New York: Norton.

Watzlawick, P.; Weakland, J.; and Fisch, R. 1974. *Change: Principles of problem formation and problem resolution.* New York: Norton.

Weakland, J.; Fisch, R.; Watzlawick, P.; and Bodin, A. 1974. Brief therapy: Focused problem resolution. *Family Process* 13:141–168.

Weitzenhoffer, A. M., and Hilgard, E. R. 1959. *Stanford hypnotic susceptibility scale.* Palo Alto, Calif.: Consulting Psychological Press.

Wolberg, L. R. 1945. *Hypnoanalysis.* New York: Grune & Stratton.

Wolpe, J. 1973. *The practice of behavior therapy.* New York: Pergamon.

INDEX